The
Complete Guide
To Writing
Readable
User Manuals

The Complete Guide To Writing Readable User Manuals

Herman Holtz

DOW JONES-IRWIN
Homewood, Illinois 60430

This publication is designed to provide accurate and authoritative information in regard to the subject matter covered. It is sold with the understanding that neither the author nor the publisher is engaged in rendering legal, accounting, or other professional service. If legal advice or other expert assistance is required, the services of a competent professional person should be sought.

From a Declaration of Principles jointly adopted by a Committee of the American Bar Association and a Committee of Publishers.

Acquisitions editor: Jim Childs
Project editor: Lynne Basler
Production manager: Carma W. Fazio
Artist: Carrie Spain
Compositor: Carlisle Communications, Ltd.
Typeface: 11/13 Century Schoolbook
Printer: Arcata/Kingsport

Library of Congress Cataloging-in-Publication Data

Holtz, Herman.
    The complete guide to writing readable user manuals / Herman R. Holtz.
      p.   cm.
    Bibliography: p.
    Includes index.
    ISBN 1-556-23097-4
    1. Electronic data processing documentation. 2. Technical writing.   I. Title.
QA76.9.D6H67 1988
005.1′5—dc19   88–5890

Printed in the United States of America

1 2 3 4 5 6 7 8 9 0 KP 5 4 3 2 1 0 9 8

Preface

The major reason for writing this book is the need for better user's instructions, better manuals. This need grows steadily more acute as our society becomes increasingly dependent on complex high-tech products and sophisticated systems.

The shortcomings in such instructions have become legendary, the butt of much bitter humor. Manufacturers and other originators of products and services are faced with the demand for improvement in this arena. Two major disasters, the crash of an Air Force fighter plane and the destruction of a space vehicle on a Cape Canaveral launch pad, were reportedly the result of inadequate user instructions.

This book addresses two classes of readers. One is those normally charged with the actual writing of user instructions, usually not professional writers, but pressed into service as writers. The other class is management, those responsible to see to it that user instructions—manuals—are created, but who are not professionals in the field of publications and editorial work. The management class may not appreciate the need for planning and methodology, or know how to go about getting such work done effectively.

Why is the subject so important? Aside from the disasters that can result from poor documentation, consider the business economics side. From the marketing viewpoint, it is in the seller's direct interest to produce first-class user manuals: Customers judge the goods and services they buy by their experiences with these manuals. If the assembly, installation, or operating instructions are unclear and the buyer has resulting difficulties, it is the product or service that is condemned.

One example is becoming painfully more familiar to many of us: the user manuals furnished with software programs for desktop computers. Software publishers are bitterly condemned by users if they fail to "support" their software adequately. And support in that field means supplying help to users who get stuck using the software because they do not understand the written explanations and instructions. Many software publishers maintain toll-free telephone lines that tie up their technical experts answering distress calls and writing letters. That's an expensive remedy for a common problem of inadequate user manuals. It makes good sense economically and in terms of customer good will to attack the problem directly by improving the manuals, rather than attacking the symptoms.

The problem and the need for a solution is growing steadily, as more items are sold in knocked-down form, requiring customer assembly or installation. Goods and services are becoming more highly technological, and require additional guidance in operating and maintaining them. Technical publishing has become a multibillion dollar industry in itself, supporting the high-tech programs of the military organizations, NASA, and other such buyers of costly and complex systems. Corporations supplying such systems often have large publishing departments of their own. Smaller companies (even the larger ones, when they encounter peaks and overloads) often turn to independent technical-publications organizations that specialize in supplying personnel and services to create user manuals and the other documentation (drawings, training programs) required. This is not the solution for the manufacturer of knocked-down, assemble-it-yourself furniture, household gadgets, and appliances. These items require user documentation, often translated from technical language into lay terms, but not on a scale that would justify calling on one of the technical-publications specialists.

Building an in-house capability for turning out first-class user manuals is becoming increasingly more practical as a direct result of desktop computers, ancillary hardware, and complementing software programs. Today, anyone can turn to the computer to produce highly professional illustrations, layouts, typesetting, page makeup, and do many other production chores. These modern systems also provide computer help with planning, outlining, spelling, proofreading, reorganizing text, and numerous other editorial chores—you can even get computer help in measuring readability levels and achieving the proper ones.

Despite all these modern marvels of this age of information and automation, the human brain must still provide the original thought, analyze the need, and do the planning. It is my hope that in these pages you will find help with that aspect of the work.

Herman R. Holtz

Contents

be defined. How much detail does the reader need? User instructions as training. Writing styles and formats.

List of Figures and Outlines

Outline

Chapter 1

Definitions and Assessments

Having lost sight of our goal, we are doubling our efforts.

BEGINNING DEFINITIONS

The word *manual* conjures up an image of a bound book, and voluminous user instructions often require binding—sometimes in multivolume sets when they are developed for the users of large systems. At the other extreme are the user instructions printed on a single sheet of paper, or contained among other information on a label or wrapping that guide the user in a simple task, such as assembling a plastic flower-pot stand or fastening a simple appliance to the wall. The difference between these is of scale or scope, but not of kind. For our purposes, *user manuals* refer to all and any kind of user instruction, regardless of the size of the physical product. Most of the information and suggestions are presented in the reference frame of large bound manuals, but many of the recommendations made here are overblown for general use, and the presumption is that you will adapt the recommendations to your specific needs, even for writing a one-page "manual."

I have used two terms here: *user manuals* and *user instructions*. The third term you may encounter, especially in dealing with government programs, is *documentation*. That term is much broader in scope and includes user instructions or manuals among written items, such as reports and contract specifications, and records in other forms than on paper, such as computer tapes and disks. (In some cases today, user manuals also appear in that form.)

One more item requires clarification: Typically, user manuals are conceived as being written about physical products. That is not always the case. In today's increasingly service-oriented economy, user manuals are often for intangibles—services such as access to online databases, use of long-distance telephone services, and operation of computer software. What is written in these pages applies equally to user manuals about physical products and services.

A BASIC FALLACY

One obstacle impeding the development of better user manuals is that we refer to *writing* user manuals, as though the ability to use the language well in writing is the key necessity in producing good user manuals. That is not the case at all; writing per se is only a portion of the task, not more than one half at best, and it is not the more important portion. I have more than one well-written manual explaining computer software programs I own, but I still have great difficulty in solving an occasional hardware or software problem because the author of the manual failed to anticipate my need for certain details.

PREPARATION TO WRITE

Is it the author's responsibility to anticipate my problems? Certainly it is. The purpose of the manual is to guide me in using the hardware or software about which the manual is written, and that includes steering me through the shoals.

The problem is a rush to the pen (an allegorical pen, of course), a rush to begin writing before planning in detail, apparently before planning at all, in some cases, and perhaps even without truly critical review and revision—without proper *preparation* to begin writing. You cannot set out to build a house without plans, improvising the design along the way with whatever ideas occurred as you proceeded!

This lack of preparation is what makes writing so difficult for many. Without proper planning, the problem is not one of how to write well, but of what to write about—what subjects to present and what to say about them. (Of course, the converse is true: with proper preparation, writing becomes much easier.)

Therefore, before moving on with specific information and suggestions for creating user manuals, this brief introduction and suggested guide to planning and preparation is offered.

KEY PLANNING ELEMENTS TO BE DEFINED IN ADVANCE

Key elements must be defined before beginning to write any user manual, no matter what its size or scope. The author must know the purpose of the manual (assembly, installation, maintenance, etc.) and the identity of the user or reader for whom it is intended. It is a practice in well-organized technical-publications groups to develop an actual profile of the reader, defining the reader's general knowledge of the subject, reading abilities, and duties or job description relevant to the manual (radar technician, computer operator, machinist).

NEEDS ASSESSMENT

After identifying the general goal or purpose of a given manual, that identification must be further developed into a detailed definition of the user's *needs* vis-à-vis the item, and here the characteristics of the item itself must be taken into account. Planning must include research in an iterative mode and research into the characteristics of the item should result in feedback to the outline of content.

A FIRST STEP

A generalized outline is offered here to identify the possible items to be considered in planning and preparation. A more detailed outline, developed from this, will be presented after a brief discussion of the preliminary outline and its use.

    I. Identify characteristics and needs.
        A. Item characteristics.
            1. Technical.
            2. Nontechnical.
        B. Item needs.
            1. Assembly.
            2. Installation.
            3. Operating procedures.
            4. Maintenance.
        C. User characteristics.
            1. Lay users.
            2. Qualified users.
        D. User needs.
            1. Assembly instructions.
            2. Operating instructions.
            3. Maintenance instructions.
            4. Technical/functional descriptions.
            5. Special training.
   II. Sort and merge.
        A. Correlate and combine characteristics and needs.
        B. Organize into order of priority.
 III. Define major chapters or manuals.
 IV. Develop preliminary (general) outlines for each.
   V. Estimate size of each.
 VI. Draft preliminary design.

DEVELOPING PRELIMINARY DATA

Developing preliminary data based on this outline can be done by an individual or by a team, depending on the overall size and scope of the project. It can be done before the first planning meeting or as a result of and follow-up to that first meeting. At the minimum, the plan for doing this ought to be presented at the first meeting, and the business of that first meeting ought to be to discuss this and select the team to work on it. It is also possible to do some of this—probably the first three major items—in advance of the meeting.

In any case, it is far better to convene that first meeting with a clear and concrete goal, such as assigning a team to work on this initial planning, than to have a general meeting for general discussion. The latter type of meeting rarely accomplishes much, except to reveal that no one really has any clear ideas for getting started on the project. There are often a far greater number of opinions being expressed than there are attendees at these first meetings—another not-very-helpful factor.

The outline shown reveals the basic strategy and the general logic of the proposed methodology for developing a total needs profile and provides a sound basis for design of the documentation and definition of the necessary content. It is actually a working blueprint as it stands, but it still calls for a great deal of estimating based on personal judgments, and the goal here is to make the process as objective and methodical as possible. The following outline is an expansion of the original, general outline. It still calls for individual judgment and estimates, but adds benchmarks or reference points to aid you in making those judgments and furthers progress toward objectivity and method. (This is only a model and/or checklist—you can adapt or improve on it as necessary and appropriate.)

I. Identify characteristics and needs.
   A. Item characteristics.
      1. Technical.
         a. Complex and/or state-of-the-art technology.
         b. Classic, medium complexity.
         c. Moderately complex.
         d. Conventional technology, not complex.
         e. Involves single technology.
         f. Spans two or more technologies.
      2. Nontechnical.
         a. Complexity of many elements, parts, applications, etc.
         b. Medium complexity of elements, parts, applications, etc.
         c. Simple, not complex.
   B. Item needs.
      1. Assembly.
         a. Complex assembly, requires many tools, special skills.
         b. Moderately difficult assembly, no special tools or skills.
         c. Simple assembly, requires only simple hand tools and skills.
      2. Installation.
         a. Complex, technological installation problems.
         b. Moderately complex, technological installation requirements.
         c. Simple, nontechnical installation requirements.

3. Operating procedures.
   a. Technological and complex, specialized procedures.
   b. Moderately technical procedures.
   c. Simple, nontechnical procedures.
4. Maintenance.
   a. Preventive.
      (1) Many routine, periodic procedures.
      (2) Requires technical knowledge.
      (3) No special knowledge required.
   b. Corrective.
      (1) Complex troubleshooting required.
      (2) Knowledge and use of special tools.
      (3) Conventional, nonspecial methods and tools.
C. User characteristics.
   1. Lay users.
      a. Novices.
      b. Expert hobbyists.
   2. Qualified users.
      a. Highly trained experts, similar item.
      b. Highly trained experts, both/all technologies.
      c. Highly trained experts, single/main technology.
      d. Moderately trained technician, similar item.
      e. Moderately trained technician both/all technologies.
      f. Moderately trained technician single/main technology.
D. User needs.
   1. Assembly instructions.
      a. General guidance.
      b. Detailed (cookbook) procedures.
      c. Special training.
   2. Operating instructions.
      a. General guidance.
      b. Detailed (cookbook) procedures.
      c. Special training.
   3. Maintenance instructions.
      a. General guidance.
      b. Detailed (cookbook) procedures.
      c. Special training.
   4. Technical/functional descriptions.
II. Sort and merge.
   A. Correlate and combine characteristics and needs.
      1. Match item needs with user needs.
      2. Develop single set of needs.
   B. Organize into order of priority.
      1. Estimate which needs most critical.
      2. Sort in descending order of priority.
III. Define major chapters or manuals.
   A. Assembly.
   B. Installation.
   C. Functional theory.
   D. Preventive maintenance.

       E. Corrective maintenance.
       F. Troubleshooting.
       G. Overhaul and repair.
       H. Parts list.
       I. Training.
  IV. Develop preliminary (general) outlines for each.
   V. Estimate size of each.
       A. Number of text pages.
       B. Number, sizes of illustrations.
       C. Number, sizes of tables.

FIGURE 1–1   Item Characteristics and Needs Worksheet

THE ITEM

Characteristics
Name: _____ [   ] Technical   [   ] Nontechnical
Brief description: _____
Technology/technologies: _____
Degree of complexity: _____
Normally delivered to user [   ] Assembled   [   ] Unassembled

Needs
Difficulty of assembly [   ] High   [   ] Moderate   [   ] Simple
Requires special tools [   ] Yes   [   ] No
Requires installation [   ] Yes   [   ] No   Requires adjustment [   ] Yes   [   ] No
Complexity of installation [   ] High   [   ] Moderate   [   ] Simple
Requires special tools [   ] Yes   [   ] No
Requires operating procedures [   ] Yes   [   ] No
Complexity of operating procedures [   ] High   [   ] Moderate   [   ] Simple
Requires preventive maintenance [   ] Yes   [   ] No
Requires corrective maintenance [   ] Yes   [   ] No
Complexity of maintenance [   ] High   [   ] Moderate   [   ] Simple
Requires special tools [   ] Yes   [   ] No
Requires detailed functional theory information [   ] Yes   [   ] No

_____

Notes

_____
_____
_____
_____

Instructions
Cross out items that do not apply. Use Notes section for additional information.

_____

VI. Draft preliminary design.
   A. Single volume.
   B. Multi-volume set.
   C. Formats.

You can, of course, reduce the scope of this outline or carry it to even more detailed levels if your situation warrants it. You might wish to note, for example, whether assembly involves special handling, installation requires delicate adjustments, maintenance requires laboratory-quality instruments or precise measurements, and whether there are major safety hazards involved anywhere. In fact, you can devise special forms (worksheets) for sketching the profile, based on transferring the information you develop from the detailed outline—which is really more

FIGURE 1–2 User Characteristics and Needs Worksheet

THE USER

Characteristics
General description or job title if appropriate: _____

_____

[ ] Lay person [ ] Novice [ ] Expert
[ ] Qualified specialist [ ] Highly trained [ ] Moderately trained
[ ] In general/main technology [ ] In related technology
[ ] In similar item

Needs (vis-a-vis item)
[ ] Assembly instructions: [ ] General [ ] Highly detailed [ ] Training
[ ] Installation instructions: [ ] General [ ] Highly detailed [ ] Training
[ ] Operating instructions: [ ] General [ ] Highly detailed [ ] Training
[ ] Functional theory: [ ] General [ ] Highly detailed [ ] Training
[ ] Preventive maintenance: [ ] General [ ] Highly detailed [ ] Training
[ ] Corrective maintenance: [ ] General [ ] Highly detailed [ ] Training
[ ] Overhaul and repair: [ ] General [ ] Highly detailed [ ] Training

Notes

_____

_____

_____

_____

_____

_____

Instructions
Cross out items that do not apply. Use Notes section for additional information.

_____

of a checklist to provoke your analytical thinking than an outline. Figures 1–1 through 1–3 are suggested models of such worksheets, based on the outline, but adaptable to designing worksheets that suit your own needs and situation. The same consideration applies to all terms used: Use the terms from the outline as guidelines for making out the worksheets or establish your own terms if you prefer.

FIGURE 1–3   Documentation Estimating Worksheet

THE DOCUMENTATION

Major Chapters/Manuals		Miscellaneous
[ ] Assembly	[ ] Preventive maintenance	[ ] Parts lists
[ ] Installation	[ ] Corrective maintenance	[ ] Training syllabus
[ ] Functional theory	[ ] Overhaul and repair	[ ] Recommended spares

Illustrations and Estimated Numbers
[ ] Assembly drawings: _____   [ ] Exploded views: _____
[ ] Schematics: _____   [ ] Plan views: _____
[ ] Illustrated parts breakdowns: __   [ ] Pictorials: _____

Estimates
Number of text pages for:
Assembly: _____   Preventive maintenance: _____
Installation: _____   Corrective maintenance: _____
Functional theory: _____   Overhaul and repair: _____
Training materials: _____   Miscellaneous: _____

Notes

_____

_____

_____

_____

_____

Instructions
Cross out items that do not apply. Use Notes section for additional information.

_____

Why User Instructions Are Needed Today: An Indoctrination

We live in an age where the art of documentation—the development of literature for the guidance of the user—has lagged behind almost everything else. The problems are classic and several, such as trying to choose between writing talent without technical knowledge and its reverse, which is often the only choice offered.

A MODERN PROBLEM

It is increasingly a do-it-yourself world today; it is also a do-it-yourself-if-you-can-figure-out-how-to-do-it world. Except for truly major and/or minor items, almost everything you buy today will be delivered as parts and fasteners in one or more corrugated-pasteboard cartons. Even more likely, you will carry it home taped to the top of your car or stuffed into the trunk with the lid open. There will be a crumpled sheet of assembly instructions stuffed into a little plastic bag with the nuts, bolts, washers, and some other little metal or plastic items. Moreover, you will never unravel the mystery of what some of those parts are for. You are more likely to be talking to yourself, trying to figure them out. (What do you call them? What are they for? Do they belong to some other product this manufacturer makes? How did they wind up in your cardboard carton? Never mind, the thing seems to hold together without them, even if it does seem just a little bit lopsided on the southern end. Maybe it's supposed to be that way. . . .) Even the rather simple electric broom my wife bought recently came in a carton with instructions for assembly. And installation instructions can be equally cryptic or misleading, however unintentionally.

MUST CUSTOMERS BECOME ENGINEERS?

The problem exists with regard to instructions for the most everyday and classical items; even a simple lamp needs assembly or partial assembly. But consider the many things we buy today, even for ordinary uses, that are high-tech products. We must master special instructions for setting digital watches and clocks because they are also calendars, joggers' stopwatches, egg timers, and calculators. The telephones we buy at Sears and K mart have automatic dialing and even clocks—if you can figure out how to work the pushbutton sequences to set the numbers into memory. Ordinary typewriters have memory circuits (they are not very ordinary anymore). And those videocassette recorders that have become so ubiquitous are almost as difficult to fathom and cope with as modern automobiles. (I have long since given up doing any of my own service on my automobile.)

Many of us feel as though an engineering degree is necessary to cope with the most common of everyday problems. (How did we ever manage before everything became so automated?) But it is not only with high-tech products that we experience this problem; it is far more common than that.

WE CALL IT DOCUMENTATION

Documentation, the creation of literature that records and explains products, has long been a problem, and it grows steadily more acute as our knowledge expands and our industry produces ever more sophisticated and complex products. In earlier times the designer of a new technical product that required user instructions wrote those instructions when the design was complete and the product was turned over to manufacturing, and to some extent that is still a practice today. But except for the simplest products, that has become a less and less practicable method. A new individual developed who specialized in technical writing—the development of literature for installation, operation, and maintenance of the equipment. Typical products requiring the services of professional technical writers for documentation are modern automotive vehicles, aircraft, radar sets, missile systems, satellites, space systems, and computers. But the problem is not confined to these situations alone. Consumers struggling with modern appliances and assembling furniture often need more help than they get.

A FEW EXAMPLES

The scope of the problem is best understood by a few specific examples.

Installing Chimes

A set of chimes came in a box with installation instructions. The box and instructions were emblazoned with warnings that a 16-volt transformer was required. But the chimes worked satisfactorily and quite safely on the existing 12-volt transformer that had been activating the buzzer that I was replacing with chimes. The warning should have read that a transformer of *not more than a maximum* 16-volt output should be used. Those who have not been trained in electrical basics would hasten to replace the existing transformer, of course, and might think it necessary to hire an electrician to install the chimes.

The Case of the Missing Parts

I once struggled most of an afternoon with a Taiwan-originated ceiling fan that would not go together as I thought it should before I realized that some of the parts were missing. Had the assembly and installation instructions been closer approximations of everyday English than they were—or had the instructions included some decent illustrations—I would probably have recognized the deficiencies much earlier. I will be most wary of that manufacturer's goods in the future.

The Tea Cart

There is, in our living room, a beautiful but defective tea cart. An Asiatic manufacturer shipped it with mounting holes drilled in the wrong places: the two ends are not identical. Because the assembly instructions were sketchy, it was not until I completed assembling it that I realized it was not exactly the same as the model in the showroom and it was a bit unbalanced; the two ends did not match precisely. The facts that (1) I could cover up the problem, more or less, by turning the cart around so that only the most critical eye would perceive the anomaly; (2) the assembly had been long and laborious and I had little enthusiasm for doing it again; (3) I had absolutely no assurance that a replacement kit would be any better than this one (it could be worse); and (4) the dealer was many miles away on the other side of the Beltway, persuaded me to forgo returning it. But that dealer will not sell me anything else, despite the fact that it is not really his fault; he, along with his supplier, must suffer the loss of my future patronage.

The Glue Gun

Nothing is ever so simple that it cannot be screwed up by a bit of carelessness. Few tools are simpler than a glue gun. This a pistol-shaped tool that melts solid glue and emits it in a fine stream for fastening things, such as wooden parts, covers of books, and plastic items. The tool is accompanied by several sticks of solid glue, and the instructions are to insert a glue stick in the gun, plug it in, and wait until the gun heats up sufficiently to melt the glue. Then press the stick forward until melted glue is dispensed. What it does not explain is that often the glue stick is not long enough to reach the tip of the gun, but this may be overcome easily by inserting a second glue stick behind the first one. I suspect that many users who are not totally at home using hand tools ponder what to do when the glue stick has passed beyond the point where it may be pressed forward by a finger. Military organizations recognize that many procedures thought up behind the comfort of a desk may not be entirely practicable or effective in the field. They therefore often require *validation* of procedures through actual tryout, but apparently few commercial manufacturers do this in developing their user instructions.

The Computer Buffer

Consider this case: A certain computer buffer that I bought for approximately $100 needs little in the way of installation; it needs to be plugged into a power outlet and to have the data cables connected, linking it to the computer on one end and the printer at the other end because it functions as an intermediary between the two units. Most of today's electronic devices, chip-based as they are, require only small amounts of voltage and current, rather than the hundreds of volts of yesterday's electronics. In the case of a great many of today's small electronic devices (e.g., calculators and computer modems) manufacturers find it is far less expensive and more practicable to employ a standard external power supply unit (a small transformer and included circuitry to convert the 110-volt household supply of alternating current to 9 volts of direct current) than to build a complex power supply into the device itself, as is done in larger devices and equipment. So this buffer comes equipped with such an external prepackaged power supply (such as you might use instead of batteries with a calculator or small tape recorder/player). The user instructions for the buffer refer to this power supply as an *adaptor*.

In explaining the installation or connection of the latter device the installation instructions dispose of the matter with these two sentences: "Plug the adaptor into the buffer's jack. Plug the adaptor into a power outlet."

The assumption is that the user will readily determine which end of the adaptor and its cable fits into the buffer jack and which end fits into the power outlet. Still, experience teaches us that many individuals would be confused by these instructions, and may not be sure what is meant by power outlet, since it is more often referred to as a receptacle. It is incomprehensible why the writer of the instructions did not write, "Connect the adaptor *between* the buffer and a power outlet" or, better yet (and more accurately), "Plug the end of the adaptor cable into the buffer jack and plug the adaptor itself into a wall receptacle," since that is literally what must be done. The adaptor is a small cubical device that has two prongs to be plugged directly into the power outlet, a common enough receptacle. But a simple little sketch would have made it even clearer so that there could have been no misunderstanding or, at least, the probability of misunderstanding would have been minimized. With computers an increasingly common household item, it is probable that the typical reader of those simple installation instructions is a lay person as far as technical knowledge is concerned. This reader does not have even a vague idea of what a jack is, or what it looks like, and might have a bit of trouble finding it on the back of the buffer, especially since it is not labeled jack, but DC9V. Those instructions should have referred to it as a jack that is labeled DC9V. And, incidentally, the instructions did not specify that the jack was on the rear panel of the buffer. A good sketch of the front panel of the buffer was included, but for some unfathomable reason no sketch of the back panel was provided, and there are four elements of importance on the back panel: the on-off switch, the two data-connector jacks, and the DC9V jack.

SOFTWARE MANUALS: THE NEWEST ENTRY

The manuals produced by the computer software industry are often singled out for popular derision with respect to incomprehensibility. Many brilliant professionals, including computer software specialists, can handle and solve intricate problems as a daily routine, but seem unable to explain their products and the instructions for using them in terms that the average user can grasp and apply. The developers of major programs and operating systems provide substantial volumes of information with their program disks, often handsomely bound in more than one volume. (The set of manuals for the new *Professional WordStar*® 4.0 impressed me almost as much as the program itself did.) Nevertheless, bookstore shelves are loaded with books written by experts other than those who created the programs, explaining all that users want and ought to know about *WordStar*®, dBase III, MS DOS, and hundreds of other popular programs and operating systems. These books sell briskly to the baffled owners of the original manuals who have been unable, somehow, to ferret out the needed instructions in the original tome. (I know the problem well. I have often been the baffled user frantically thumbing the dog-eared pages of the original manuals in utter despair of ever uncovering the answers I am seeking. I have purchased many books that explained my major programs and operating systems when I could not find the answers I sought in the original manuals.)

IT IS A TOWER OF BABEL

Some of the knockdown items that must be assembled are simple enough (for the "handy" householder), but even the simplest assembly may baffle an individual who is brilliant in presenting arguments to a jury, managing a complex corporate merger, or finding a missing person.

Many highly gifted individuals simply lack that critical melange of tool-using skill, manual dexterity, and almost instinctive grasp of spatial relationships so necessary to being what is casually described as "handy with tools." And even those who have such gifts usually need a bit of help—user instructions—to fathom what the designer had in mind for all the strange-looking parts and fasteners. The language problem—the problem of technical jargon and technical terms—enters into it also, even when the terms appear simple. Not everyone knows what a Phillips screwdriver or Allen wrench is. The problem is not confined to those whose professions and skills are unrelated to tool-using ones; even those who, we presume, ought to have the requisite knowledge may not have it. I once sought, in vain and in utter frustration, to find a hardware store where the clerks knew what a spline wrench is, and had one to sell me. The IBM typewriter-service technician carries at least one spline wrench to tighten a fastener on the platen (which is what I wanted the wrench for). I finally had to call on IBM to do this simple job because I never did find anyone in this area who even knew what they were! Imagine the agony you could cause a customer by specifying a need for such a tool without explaining further!

SOME REASONS FOR THE PROBLEM

The problem exists with user instructions of all kinds, possibly because writing instructions comes as an afterthought. Often the reluctant designer is required to write these instructions and writing may be considered an unpleasant chore that is disposed of as quickly as possible.

Problems of this kind are so common that, in fact, it has become a premise that few professionals write well and most dislike writing intensely. Perhaps that is why they do not write well. The reverse could be true: Perhaps they dislike writing because they have not learned to write well, and thus have found writing to be a far more onerous task than it might otherwise be. In any case, this has long been a problem in all technological fields, leading (along with such other factors as the growing complexity of modern products) to the rise of technical writing as a profession in itself. (It began in Detroit, writing service manuals for automobiles.) The growing need for writing skills in the engineering professions has led to required courses in writing in many engineering schools, and technical writing is itself a major in some schools.

Today there are both career technical writers and technical-writing consultants, most of whom are engineers or experienced technicians. I was one of a half dozen such consultants called in by Remington-Rand to edit, rewrite, and otherwise repair their manuals on the LARC computer so the U.S. Navy would accept the manuals (which they had rejected in their original version) and pay their bill. Technical writing has become an industry in itself, spawning many companies devoted primarily to providing technical-writing services, technical-writing temporary personnel, and technical-writing consultative services. Principally, these companies specialize in developing technical manuals and related documentation for high-technology manufacturers, especially those whose products are developed for, and under contract to, military organizations. For military units, dependent as they are on their enlisted personnel to install, operate, and maintain modern high-tech systems, utility of the documentation is of critical importance and they have developed and are still developing many detailed specifications to guide those who write the manuals and related documentation. The Department of Defense is largely responsible for the rise of technical writing as the result of many massive projects requiring the development of multi-volume documentation. For example, an Air Force project for a massive logistics/communication program (*465L* in military jargon) required the production of 35 volumes averaging 1,000 pages each, and IBM kept approximately 30 technical writers busy on the project for many months translating the engineering data into user information and originating much additional information required to meet user needs.

THE TECHNICAL-WRITING DILEMMA

A classic problem in technical writing is that two separate qualifications, writing skills and technological knowledge, are required. And the technologies have become so complex and specialized that it is not enough to be a technical writer or even an electronics technical writer; employers today often stipulate even more detailed qualifications as their requirements, such as "radar writers," "computer writers," "communications writers." Some even insist that they will hire only writers familiar with some given military specification for a certain type of manual (for the military have many specifications for documentation, as well as for equipment and services).

On the other hand, some organizations have tended to broader terms, such as "maintenance writers," "manuals writers" and "documentations specialists," or even simply "experienced writers." (There are many kinds of specialists in the general writing world too, and those who would be most likely to tend to this kind of writing are known or think of themselves as "how to" writers.)

The dilemma is simple enough to state: Should the individual assigned to documentation be a technical expert who must learn to write, or an experienced writer who can manage through research and consultation with technical experts to produce suitable documentation? Certainly it cannot be easy, if it is even possible or practicable, to write a highly technical manual about a highly technical equipment, if the writer has absolutely no technical training in the subject. Even with the availability of technical experts for consultation it takes at least a minimum of technical education to understand the language of the technologies involved and to do the research effectively.

It appears more sensible to pursue the first course since, presumably, every educated individual has been schooled in using our language in writing, as well as in speech. Therefore, in theory at least, engineers and technicians should have little difficulty in learning to write manuals and other documentation, especially with the aid of style guides, specifications, and editing support. (And especially if they acknowledge that they must *learn* the art or craft of technical writing—that it does involve methodology and method more than art.) The majority of technical writers today are engineers and technicians who have learned something of manuals writing, and the editors are generally English majors and/or qualified writers, albeit often not technical experts. (That is itself sometimes an advantage for it is often helpful to have someone ask the "dumb questions!") But most technical writers are not creative writers and are not driven by the need for self-expression. Hence, they practice a trade or craft, not an art. It is thus absolutely necessary to create principles, rules, procedures, and standards to make it work at all. And, these technical writers must also understand some of the principles that guide all writers.

WHO IS RESPONSIBLE FOR UNDERSTANDING THE INSTRUCTIONS?

It's true that there are some individuals who never "get the word," as some people in the U.S. Navy say, no matter what pains you go to in trying to make misunderstanding impossible. But that is not a proper excuse for failing to make all reasonable efforts to make it easier to understand than to misunderstand.

The first priority is where and on whom the prime responsibility for understanding falls: It falls on the writer, not on the reader. For example, an editor in a technical-manuals project once called me to task for my use of the word *epitome,* where I had remarked that the arithmetic unit of the computer is the epitome of computer operation generally. I was puzzled at first by the complaint because I was certain that I had used that word quite correctly. The suspicion came to me gradually that the editor did not himself understand the precise definition of that term—it does have a subtle shading—and thus did not understand its proper application at all. I persuaded the editor to look the word up, received his embarrassed apology, and returned to work. But I was still troubled with a vague unease about the matter, although I was not sure why. I soon reasoned out what was still bothering me when I turned to several other writers whose opinions and abilities I respected and asked them to define the word for me. That crystallized my problem: not one of them knew the *precise* definition—they all had only vague ideas as to its approximate meaning—and could not, therefore, have used that word appropriately, much less judged whether I had done so.

I immediately—and most regretfully—edited that word out of my copy and found another term to use, a synonym not quite as right for the purpose, but one that most readers would probably understand. Checking with experienced writers had demonstrated clearly to me that few people would be likely to have a full and accurate understanding of that word if so few professional writers know the word well enough to use it.

The point is, of course, that being right is not important and is certainly not the issue; being understood is the issue, and it is what must have the first priority.

THE WRITER'S TOOLS

All writers need tools to do their job, just as anyone practicing a profession or trade does. They must learn what the tools are and how and where to use them. But it is easy to miss the obvious tools.

Some years ago, as manager of an organization devoted to writing manuals and training programs, among other products and services, I discovered a little practical test that I found to be most helpful in hiring writers for a fast-growing staff. I first screened out those applicants who appeared to meet none of my predetermined qualifications. I then asked those applicants whose resumes made them appear to be suitably qualified to explain in writing, in not more than 100 words, how to write a personal check. The reader was specified as someone who was completely unfamiliar with the entire concept of a check, so that the writer could take absolutely nothing for granted but had to explain every detail of the process. Remember in reading the following that each of these candidates was a writer with some degree of professional experience in writing; none was a student or beginner.

The results of this little test were always interesting. Most applicants found it difficult to cover the subject adequately in so few words unless they started from the premise that the reader at least knew what a check was. But every now and then one of the applicants managed to do the job adequately with words to spare—using as few as 50 or 60 words!

How did these latter writers finesse the problem so easily? Quite simply: They understood that their true mission was to *communicate*, not to write, using *all* the tools available to the imaginative writer. The other applicants all thought of themselves as wordsmiths only, individuals who knew and could use a wide variety of words. The few, rare applicants who mastered the test so aptly were those who had the wit to first draw a little sketch of a check already made out and then write their explanation with reference to the sketch. The rest was easy!

That points up just one of the many problems with user instructions: Too many writers have the notion that their craft is confined to the use of words alone and use illustrations only as an afterthought, appending the illustrations to the text instead of basing the explanation on the drawing or photograph. In short, they illustrate their words instead of illustrating the concept. They forget that words are only symbols and are not nearly as effective as graphic illustrations in communicating many images and ideas. In technical writing especially, graphics and other types of illustration are one of the most valuable tools, if not the most valuable.

One common cause for confusion among householders today is the profusion of electrical plugs for household appliances and other electrical goods. There are still many of the old two-prong plugs and matching wall receptacles in use, but the newer polarized plugs, won't fit the old receptacles. And there are two types of polarized plugs. One type has two prongs, one prong wider than the other, and a second type has three prongs. Figure 2–1 illustrates a simple way to cope with the problem by offering the user a simple line drawing showing how to use

FIGURE 2–1 Line Drawing of Electrical Plug and Adaptor

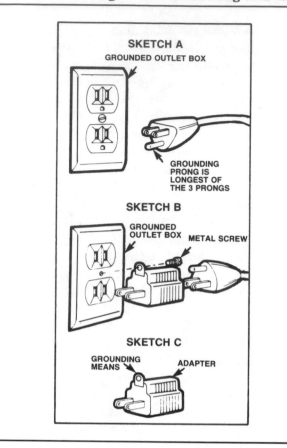

Courtesy Black & Decker, Inc.

an adapter between the old-fashioned wall receptacle and either of the newer plugs. Text accompanies this illustration, of course.

Figure 2–2 is another example of simple line art to handle the bulk of the information exchange needed.

Photographs, drawings, and charts are helpful, but they are not the only kinds of illustrations that can be resorted to and that prove helpful. Ideas are also often illustrated—even *illuminated*—by such writers' imagery as analogies, metaphors, and similes. It is perfectly accurate and correct to explain that the earth is an oblate spheroid, but those words would send a great many readers to the dictionary and cause many others to sigh and turn to something else. But most would have no difficulty in visualizing the earth as "round and flattened slightly at each end, like an orange," because most of us are quite familiar with oranges. If there is some good reason to use the more technical and abstract term *oblate spheroid,* a simple line drawing illustrating what that term means would be equally satisfactory.

Some concepts cannot be illustrated so easily, even by metaphors, similes, or drawings, but that does not mean that something cannot be done to help the reader. There are analogies that can be devised to help a reader understand an abstraction about an unfamiliar proposition.

FIGURE 2–2 Line Drawings of Electric Iron

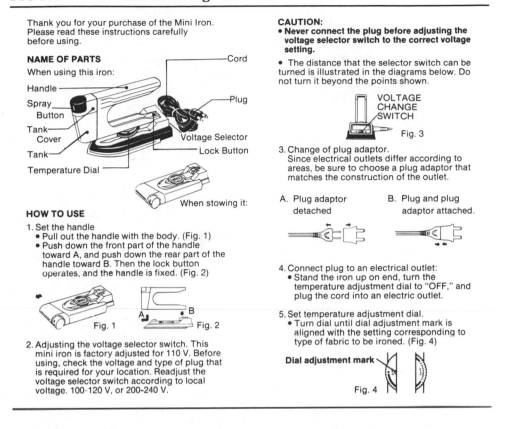

Thank you for your purchase of the Mini Iron. Please read these instructions carefully before using.

NAME OF PARTS

When using this iron:

Handle
Spray Button
Tank Cover
Tank
Temperature Dial
Cord
Plug
Voltage Selector
Lock Button

When stowing it:

HOW TO USE

1. Set the handle
   • Pull out the handle with the body. (Fig. 1)
   • Push down the front part of the handle toward A, and push down the rear part of the handle toward B. Then the lock button operates, and the handle is fixed. (Fig. 2)

Fig. 1   Fig. 2

2. Adjusting the voltage selector switch. This mini iron is factory adjusted for 110 V. Before using, check the voltage and type of plug that is required for your location. Readjust the voltage selector switch according to local voltage. 100-120 V, or 200-240 V.

CAUTION:
• **Never connect the plug before adjusting the voltage selector switch to the correct voltage setting.**

• The distance that the selector switch can be turned is illustrated in the diagrams below. Do not turn it beyond the points shown.

VOLTAGE CHANGE SWITCH

Fig. 3

3. Change of plug adaptor.
   Since electrical outlets differ according to areas, be sure to choose a plug adaptor that matches the construction of the outlet.

A. Plug adaptor detached
B. Plug and plug adaptor attached.

4. Connect plug to an electrical outlet:
   • Stand the iron up on end, turn the temperature adjustment dial to "OFF," and plug the cord into an electric outlet.

5. Set temperature adjustment dial.
   • Turn dial until dial adjustment mark is aligned with the setting corresponding to type of fabric to be ironed. (Fig. 4)

Dial adjustment mark

Fig. 4

Many technical writers fail to make use of matrices and tables to aid understanding and offer a more efficient presentation. In one case where a technical writer had written almost endlessly repetitive narrative describing a series of maintenance procedures a consultant converted these to a matrix. That reduced the sheer bulk of verbiage to a fraction of the original draft, and simplified the problem of understanding the material. The matrix format is inherently more efficient than narrative because it reveals and dramatizes common factors.

The technical writer was astonished. He had, for some reason, assumed that only numbers and symbols were suitable for tabular organization, and so it had never occurred to him that the narratives could be assembled into groups and blocks of text with common characteristics and organized into a table or matrix.

THERE MAY BE A LITERACY PROBLEM ALSO

One of our more stubborn problems is that of illiteracy. Literacy or illiteracy is not a black-and-white proposition, but exists in stages or degrees of literacy. (In the Job Corps experience the term *functionally illiterate* gained great currency to describe those who read haltingly and with extremely limited vocabularies.) This has taken a curious twist in modern times and become something of a phenomenon. Even well-educated people today are often less than totally literate: they read poorly, despite high school diplomas and even college degrees. We are still largely a nation of immigrants, and so we have many among us who are not highly literate in English, although they may be quite literate in their native languages. We must always consider this factor, especially when writing instructions concerning ordinary consumer goods.

TECHNICAL WRITING DOES NOT HAVE TO BE STULTIFYING

I had the temerity once to begin a technical manual about a technologically advanced missile system—the tracking and guidance radar equipment in the system was of revolutionary design—with a writer's tactic calculated to gain the reader's attention and arouse interest immediately. I did this by presenting a summation of the system's near-miraculous capabilities and the promise that pages to follow would explain in detail how these marvels were accomplished by this breakthrough design in radar technology.

A design engineer assigned to conduct technical review of my manuscript condemned it with the surly observation, "It reads like a [expletive deleted] novel," which he obviously intended as a scathing denunciation.

This individual neglected his proper task—technical review—to pass judgment gratuitously on that for which he was unqualified—editorial merit. That alone is a problem in technical publications; it seems that everyone wants to be an editor and thinks himself or herself qualified for the task. In their eagerness to impose their editorial judgment, those individuals often tend to neglect that review responsibility with which they are properly charged.

Worse, however, is this unfortunately typical attitude of many professionals, especially the technical experts whose duties involve them somehow in the development of the user manuals. Their bias is that the writing must be wooden, the pace laborious, and the exposition totally unimaginative. They surely would not recognize these as fair characterizations because they confuse formal and dignified prose—which they apparently think is essential to their professional images—with such writing. They are obviously unaware of, or indifferent to, the fact that some of the world's most eminent scientists and thinkers (e.g., the late Sir Arthur Eddington, Bertrand Russell, and George Gamow) wrote serious formal books in an enormously readable style and with brilliant humor. This attitude results in many technical publications being difficult to read and even more difficult to understand without strenuous effort. It is also a completely unnecessary and irrational bias: user instructions do not have to be ponderous and difficult to read, and there is no earthly reason that they should be so.

Consequently, one of the objectives of this book is to persuade you to the philosophy that user manuals should be written in a more popular style, and that this style will actually improve these manuals. And, of course, guidance in achieving this will be offered in these pages.

BUT IT IS NOT ENTIRELY *HOW* YOU WRITE . . . .

One serious obstacle in the way of good manuals is the universal tendency to refer to *writing* manuals as though the act of putting words on paper represents the entire task or even the major part of the task. Even when we recognize that writing includes illustrations of many kinds, graphics as well as imagery in language, we must recognize that *what* you write in a manual is even more important than *how* you write it. A well-written manual that neglects to include necessary information is not a good manual.

Recently, the calendar that is an integral part of my computer advised me that we were in the year 2005. I had no difficulty changing the date to the correct one for the remainder of that session, but when I restarted the computer on a subsequent session I found myself again in the year 2005, as far as my computer was concerned. I searched both the manufacturer's manual and an expensive one I had bought in a local bookstore for a command that would correct the computer internally and return it to the present year. All I learned was that the time and date functions reposed in a file named PC TIMER 1.3; nothing more. I found the answer eventually, but not in any of the obvious manuals. I was compelled to resort to a highly technical method the average user is not likely to be able to employ. The information should have been included in the manufacturer's literature, of course.

What to write—a complete inventory of the user's information needs—can be developed only through careful research and planning, the amount dependent primarily on the prior knowledge of the writer. It is not a simple process. It is, in fact, usually an iterative one, between the two interdependent main elements of research and planning. It begins with an assessment of the need—for whom is the manual intended and what is the user expected to be enabled to *do* with the information. That should be in as much detail as possible. There must be the development of a preliminary outline, with many iterations—more thought, more planning, research, and expansion of the outline. And that research is necessary even for the subject-matter expert, who conducts at least part of the research by exploring his or her own knowledge while expanding the outline. Each iteration of one function leads to an iteration of the other until some point where you believe you have described in your outline precisely what is to be included in the manual. Only then are you ready to begin serious writing of a first draft.

Those who are still new to the process may make the mistake of attempting to write a first draft too soon—before planning and research are complete or appear to be so. (It is not at all unusual to discover the need for more information—more research—while writing, and that additional research may make the essential difference between an excellent manual and a marginal one.) Probably at least one half the time ought to be expended in this planning and research stage, except in unusual circumstances. It is time well invested. To a large degree this is the "secret" of writing, for it is the lack of planning and preparation that makes writing difficult; with adequate planning and preparation, not only is the manual a far better product; writing it is a far easier task.

The Classes of User Manuals

The very number of types of user manuals is growing, not surprisingly; that is a direct reflection of the growing sophistication and complexity of modern technology. But there are other contributing factors.

THE BASIC USER NEEDS

User manuals must inevitably be inspired by and based on the perceived needs of users. There are several needs normally encountered by the buyers of almost all but the simplest of products:

Description
Installation
Operation
Maintenance
Training

These are the most basic and general of needs expressed in the most general terms possible. In practice—in specific cases—they vary widely, according to a wide variety of circumstances and conditions. There is the complexity of the product itself. There is the environment in which it is to be installed and used. And, there are the nature or characteristics of the user(s) and sometimes special conditions or considerations. In practice, at least for large and complex products, each of these general categories must be further broken down into subcategories. So the number of separate manuals or volumes in a given set of manuals may become quite large indeed, as in the case of the 35 large bound volumes of about 1,000 pages each in one U.S. Air Force project of a few years ago.

NATURE AND CHARACTERISTICS OF THE USERS

Users fall into classes too, and that itself is a major consideration. Who or what is the user in terms of the product in question: Is the user an average consumer? An equipment operator? A service technician? Other? The information packed with a product to be sold to an average consumer and used in an average household has far different requirements than one packed with a complex piece of machinery for use in a plant or on a military base. This complex equipment will need formal installation and regular maintenance by qualified technicians armed with suitable technical details and guidance.

That is not the only difference to consider. The military services (especially the U.S. Army because it needs to recruit and train such large numbers of men and women) are faced with the problem of training many of their enlisted people and officers in operating and maintaining increasingly large and complex equipment systems. The majority of these individuals have no prior specialized education or training in the appropriate fields so they must get some basic training in the relevant technology, as well as in the general basic training administered to every enlistee. Moreover, the vast majority of these people do not remain in the military service for a lifetime career and so the military must limit the time allowed for training. That imposes many special problems and requirements on the documentation and has resulted in requirements for and development of many special types of user documentation, such as instructions that enable personnel with limited formal training to maintain complex systems. There is also that special military problem of assembling, installing, operating, and maintaining equipment under field conditions and in emergencies, such as improvising operations at reduced capacity.

But those are not the only difference factors among users. Many consumers, even those who are high school graduates, do not read with great facility, and so education and literacy are often a consideration. Many of today's consumers are well educated and highly literate in their native culture, but read and often speak English poorly or not at all. These factors and others have a pronounced effect on the design and development of user instructions, as will become evident.

DESCRIPTION

User instructions generally describe the product, although not necessarily directly or physically. They do not necessarily use the word *description*. Depending on the size and complexity of the product, the documentation may use such terms as *characteristics,* and manuals for military equipment often present a chapter or volume titled *Theory of Operation.*

The 27-page *Owner's Manual* for a multifunctional desktop telephone sold by Sears begins with a section titled *Description* (immediately following the front matter, that is). This section is three pages long, and each page consists of a line drawing of the product with numbered lines drawn to different portions of the depicted telephone set and a listing at the bottom of the page describing what each of those lines identifies. Thirty-three items are so identified.

Theory of operation, a detailed technical discussion of the product, including design considerations and other such information, is not appropriate here, of course. This user is an average consumer and wants to know only how to set the instrument up and use it—installation and operating instructions.

Figure 3–1 illustrates this graphically. The figure is a page reproduced from a manual for a dot matrix printer, the North Atlantic Qantex

FIGURE 3–1   First Page of a Description of a Dot Matrix Printer

SECTION 1

DESCRIPTION

1.1   SCOPE

The purpose of this manual is:

- To define the printer's capability.
- To train the operator in its use.
- To show the programmer how to select the features.
- To assist the systems engineer to interface the printer with the host system.

1.2   PHYSICAL DESCRIPTION

The Model 7030 printer (fig. 1–1) is designed for simplicity of operation and service and consists essentially of the mechanical assembly, power supply, and logic board.

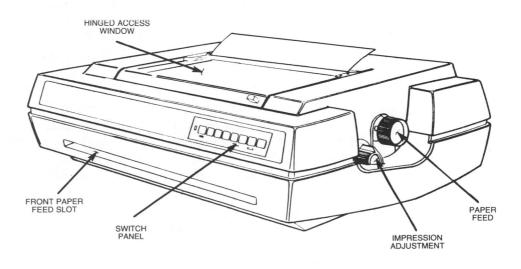

Figure 1–1 Model 7030 Printer

Reproduced through courtesy of North Atlantic Industries, Inc.

7030/7040. This page begins the first chapter of the *Operator's Manual* for the printer, and is labeled *Description*. There are several pages following with text and tabular data amplifying and filling out the description.

On the other hand the *Use & Care Guide* for a Whirlpool dishwasher does not use the word *description* at all, but describes the product in its 15-page manual headed *Parts and Features*. As in the case of the telephone use guide the description consists of a line drawing of the product with "call outs"—lines leading to different areas, each line labeled to describe what it is pointing to.

A Radio Shack telephone handset—a simple telephone with no fancy features—is accompanied by a small, 24-page *Owner's Manual* that describes the product in the first four pages under two headings: *Features,* a simple one-page listing of nine items, including a built-in amplifier, and *Controls and Functions,* listed on the next three pages via photographs of the telephone and identifications of each control and function.

Even a medium-priced Waltham conventional (dial type) wrist watch comes armed with a tiny brochure, *Watchowner's Guide,* which is more advertisement than instructions, but it does describe the watch, its features, and related facts.

But a Casio digital wrist watch comes backed with a tiny 32-page *User's Guide,* printed in type so small that I need a reading glass to make out what it says. A two-page spread following front matter, is labeled *Reading the Display* and offers a pictorial diagram of different possible displays.

The 24-page manual for a Sony videocassette recorder pursues much the idea of other manuals, with a photograph of the front of the unit and a line drawing of the rear panel and call outs identifying various controls, indicators, and terminals.

Of course, many items do have accompanying owner's guides of one sort or another, but are such common commodities that they truly need no description. Inexpensive models of pocket calculators, for example, have become commonplace to this degree, for example, and the user instructions are generally printed on the card to which they are attached.

The *User's Manual* for *Electra-Find,* a computer software program, describes the product in a first chapter titled *Introduction*. On the other hand, the *User's Guide* for *Out-Think,* another computer program, furnishes a detailed description in its first chapter, titled *Introduction,* but offers installation instructions in a separate manual of 32 pages.

All of these user instructions are intended for laypersons, (although in the case of computer software, much of the manual information is geared to users who have considerable technical knowledge, (and even these technically sophisticated users often complain about the poor quality of typical software manuals).

In all these cases the documentation is for consumer goods—goods bought by the average consumer for personal use. A consumer will usually either turn to specialists for maintenance and repair services or will discard a malfunctioning product and buy a new one. (This is becoming an increasingly popular practice in recent years, owing to a variety of considerations that makes repair of many items less and less attractive).

There is an entirely different kind of manual for the user who will be performing maintenance on the item. It is usually possible to buy separate manuals, maintenance manuals, for items normally requiring maintenance, such as automobiles, videocassette recorders, washing machines, and other such equipment. These manuals offer technical descriptions, test information, troubleshooting suggestions, parts lists, procedural guidance, and other assistance. Technical descriptions here tend to take on the theory-of-operation complexion, explaining normal operation in technical language, along with such data as design rationales. All of this is considered a necessary preparation for mastering maintenance at the troubleshooting and diagnostic levels. This is also preparation for overhaul and repair (O&R), called that to distinguish it from the less difficult maintenance tasks referred to as preventive maintenance and corrective maintenance. (Performing corrective maintenance, however, normally requires technical knowledge and troubleshooting skills also, perhaps even more than O&R does.)

Descriptions are not furnished for their own sake. They are furnished to serve specific purposes, the anticipated needs of the reader. Descriptions must thus anticipate and make provision for the other areas of documentation. Those descriptions cited here as examples were of consumer goods for which there was usually only a few setup instructions and perhaps minor assembly or other installation requirements to consider. Hence, the descriptions did not have to be elaborate, as they would be in preparing to present complex assembly, installation, and/or maintenance coverage. In most cases of small and simple consumer goods the description serves to acquaint the user with controls for operation and for assembly parts and hardware for installation.

INSTALLATION

The term *installation* was introduced and used in a most general sense, as was the general term *description,* and will be further detailed and qualified with the designation of at least two subset designators of *installation—assembly* and *setup.* But it is not a black and white world, and so there is often a rather fine shading between or among these. This compels us to arbitrarily call certain coverage by one or the other term, and so I have chosen to lump setup and assembly instructions under the general category of installation instructions.

Users do not require installation instructions for many items. The user does not expect the manufacturer to suggest installation instructions for most ordinary household items that come completely assembled or for most small appliances, such as a kitchen clock or toaster. Still, there are exceptions. For example, there is a combination clock, radio, and timer for the kitchen that comes with special brackets and mounting hardware to fasten it to the underside of the kitchen wall cabinets and so includes mounting instructions that border on, and might even qualify as, assembly instructions. And a modern toaster-oven is now being offered that is equipped for similar mounting. So even conventional, small items may require installation instructions.

Setup instructions are often needed for even small, common items—such as a digital wrist watch that requires some manipulation of dials and pushbuttons to set it or, in the case of a TV, where the setup is as simple as connecting it to an antenna. However, a TV receiver I encountered recently was designed to be connected to an outdoor antenna only, having no built-in "rabbit ears" of its own, unlike virtually all TV sets of recent years. To further complicate what appears to be a design slip-up, the instructions failed to mention that an indoor antenna could be used instead of an outdoor one, should the latter be unavailable, an incomprehensible oversight in the user instructions. (Many users would be fearful of attaching an indoor antenna without being assured that is was permissible and safe to do so.)

At the other extreme, there are systems that require extensive installation effort and documentation that includes complete manuals and special drawings. Installing an airport system for guiding planes to a safe landing, for example, is setup on a large scale, requiring a great deal of work, such as excavating and pouring foundations, assembling and erecting towers, bolting down large equipment, and testing and tuning. Such installations can take many months to complete and require hundreds, even thousands, of pages of text and diagrams to guide the installation crews, which will normally be under the supervision and guidance of qualified technical experts.

What we are discussing here is, then, a matter of scale, not of kind. The principles are the same, whether the installation covers the assembly/installation/setup of a coffee table or of a missile system. Even the difference in users—the technical expert versus the lay person—is more a difference in scale than in kind. All user instructions must be written with a presumption of some well-defined intended reader, with a clear distinction between the average consumer and the especially qualified user. That is not to say that assembly instructions written for the average consumer cannot be relatively complex; they can. But let's look first at some typical assembly instructions for a simple item.

Probably the assembly instructions shown in Figure 3–2 are near the lower end of the scale for simplicity. The device to be assembled here is a bed frame. Because what is to be assembled is a simple device, anyone who is familiar with tools and their use would have little trouble assembling the bed frame with the help of these instructions. But for the individual who is not familiar with tools and everyday hardware, the instructions might well prove to be somewhat cryptic. For example (reading instruction 1), such a user might not know just what a hex nut is. Instruction 3 requires some study to decipher even for the mechanically knowledgeable assembler.

On the other hand the assembly instructions for a more elaborate device—an outdoor children's gym, in this case—provides drawings of the tools and fastening hardware supplied so that the user has no trouble identifying the item referred to in the text and assembly drawings. Figures 3–3 and 3–4, simple line drawings of common hand tools and fasteners—different kinds of nuts, bolts, and other such devices—illus-

FIGURE 3–2   Assembly Instructions for a Bed Frame

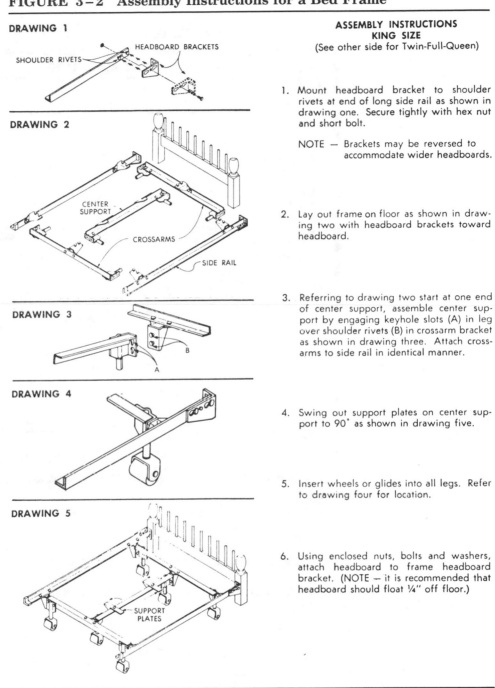

DRAWING 1

SHOULDER RIVETS

HEADBOARD BRACKETS

DRAWING 2

CENTER SUPPORT

CROSSARMS

SIDE RAIL

DRAWING 3

A   B

DRAWING 4

DRAWING 5

SUPPORT PLATES

ASSEMBLY INSTRUCTIONS
KING SIZE
(See other side for Twin-Full-Queen)

1. Mount headboard bracket to shoulder rivets at end of long side rail as shown in drawing one. Secure tightly with hex nut and short bolt.

   NOTE — Brackets may be reversed to accommodate wider headboards.

2. Lay out frame on floor as shown in drawing two with headboard brackets toward headboard.

3. Referring to drawing two start at one end of center support, assemble center support by engaging keyhole slots (A) in leg over shoulder rivets (B) in crossarm bracket as shown in drawing three. Attach crossarms to side rail in identical manner.

4. Swing out support plates on center support to 90° as shown in drawing five.

5. Insert wheels or glides into all legs. Refer to drawing four for location.

6. Using enclosed nuts, bolts and washers, attach headboard to frame headboard bracket. (NOTE — it is recommended that headboard should float ¼" off floor.)

trate this. This is almost an essential for assembly instructions designed to be used by lay people, many of whom have only a slight familiarity with common hand tools and hardware fasteners and many, many more who lack even that slight familiarity, so that they may be puzzled and frustrated by references to lag bolts or channel-grip pliers.

A sizable step further up the ladder toward the more complex installation is that represented by the installation instructions for the

FIGURE 3–3   Illustrations Identifying Fastening Hardware

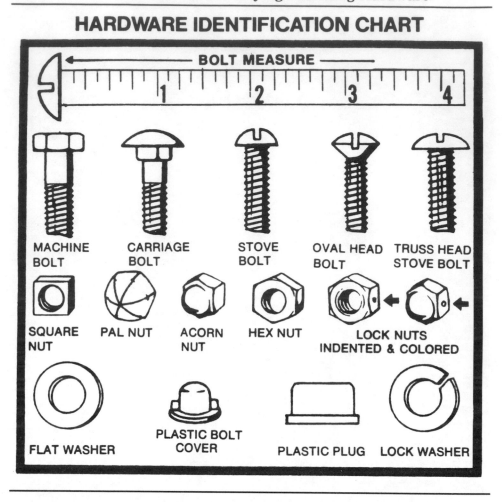

FIGURE 3–4   Illustrations Identifying Hand Tools

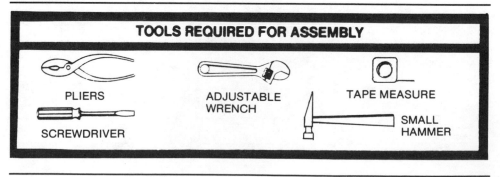

North Atlantic Qantex Model 7030/7040 computer printer, which was introduced and illustrated earlier. The installation instructions are presented in that *Operator's Manual* as Section 2, a 19-page chapter illustrated with a half-dozen line drawings similar to that shown on the first page of that chapter (see Figure 3–5) and with numerous textual explanations, procedural listings, and tables of detailed data for in-

FIGURE 3–5   First Page of an Installation Chapter

SECTION 2

INSTALLATIONS

2.1   INITIAL SET-UP

After visual inspection, perform the following procedure.

a.   Before connecting the power cord, set the 115/230 V switch (screw driver actuated on rear of printer) to the appropriate line voltage.

WARNING

Connection to the wrong power main
voltage will damage the printer.

b.   Make sure that the PWR switch on the rear of the printer chassis is in the OFF position. Insert the power cord into the selected AC outlet.

2.2   CHANGING OR INSTALLING RIBBON

Install the ribbon (see recommended ribbon source list inside printer chassis or in Appendix C) as follows (fig. 2-1):

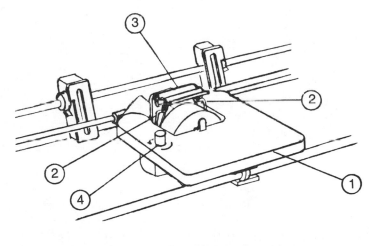

Figure 2-1. Replacing Ribbon Cartridge

Reproduced through courtesy of North Atlantic Industries, Inc.

stallation. Two of the numerous tables (there are, in fact 16 such tables) are illustrated in Figure 3–6. Note that the information furnished is somewhat technical and obviously not intended for the direct use of the lay person. This is not the typical lower-priced computer printer the buyer of a computer for private use at home is most likely to buy, but is one of the more expensive types designed for the heavy-duty commercial or industrial use, with many features not found in lower-priced models, including numerous controls, adjustments, and indicators. In

FIGURE 3–6 Tables Listing Switch Settings for Installation

2.4.4   DIP Switch SW3 Settings (Fig. 2-5)

2.4.4.1   Printing Mode

The printer operates at several Draft and Word Processing mode speeds. Table 2-11 provides DIP switch settings for the various printing modes.

Table 2-11. Printing Modes

Switch Settings		Print Mode
SW3-1	SW3-2	
CLOSED	CLOSED	180 CPS (draft mode)
OPEN	CLOSED	150 CPS (compose mode)
CLOSED	OPEN	75 CPS (word-processing, NLQ, single pass)
OPEN	OPEN	37 CPS (word processing, letter-quality, double pass)

2.4.4.2   Line Protocol

Switches SW3-3 and SW3-4 control the communications protocol of a serial interface in accordance with table 2-12.

Table 2-12. Line Protocol

Switch Settings		Line Protocol
SW-3	SW-4	
CLOSED	CLOSED	X-ON/X-OFF
OPEN	CLOSED	STX/ETX
CLOSED	OPEN	Busy is (+) true
OPEN	OPEN	Busy is (−) true

2.4.4.3   Horizontal Pitch (Characters Per Inch)

Horizontal pitch determines the width and center to center spacing of printed characters. The Model 7030 has five horizontal pitch selections (table 2-13) in the Draft and Compose modes. The Word Processing modes allow a pitch selection of 10, 12, and 13.3 characters per inch only. An attempt to select WP pitches other than those listed will force the printer into a default pitch of 13.3 characters per inch.

Reproduced through courtesy of North Atlantic Industries, Inc.

fact, despite 19 pages of data in the installation chapter of the manual, the more detailed technical data the user might require for installation of this printer are contained in a number of appendices, charts, and other presentations.

Not only furniture and hardware devices require assembly and/or installation. Any computer owner who acquires new software programs learns that most such programs require installation. The term *installation* is, in fact, used for this initial procedure, although it is quite different than assembling or installing a piece of equipment. In fact, for large programs often a full-blown installation sub-program is required, as in the case of the new *Professional WordStar 4®* program and others of equal size and importance.

Installation of new software programs generally means making necessary adjustments to make the new software totally compatible with your specific needs and situation. One major consideration is always matching the new program to your printer, for example, but it may also require matching up other hardware, such as a modem, and also setting the new program to your preferences. In installing the new *WordStar®* program, for example, I had many options, such as the type styles, margins, paragraphs, and numerous other items to be set by "default"— set automatically by the system when I turn on the computer. More and more software programs are being written to furnish a wide variety of such options and to permit the user to do most of the installation without the need to call on an expert, as was often the case with the hardware and software of only a few years ago.

The Kamasoft *OutThink* program manual is also uncharacteristically heavy in installation guidance, devoting slightly more than one half its coverage to installation procedures, largely because it combines adjusting the program to your own hardware and your own editorial preferences.

The adjustments to be made during and by installation procedures varies according to the nature of the program. Installation of a word processing program is generally concerned mostly with editing, formatting, and printer commands because that is what word processing is all about. But other kinds of programs have other kinds of concerns, such as your own individual information needs. For example, a program designed to help the user manage an investment portfolio has an installation program that focuses primarily on establishing the set of files based on your own investments. In this case you must establish an individual file for each stock, bond, or other investment you hold and create the first set of plots and evaluations, which you will update in the future when there is any kind of change to report for any of these.

Nevertheless, many users are fearful of doing software installation themselves because they are intimidated by computers, so it poses a greater problem for writers of software documentation than for writers of user manuals for furniture and hardware items. (Hand tools and mechanical operations are apparently less formidable for the average consumer.)

OPERATION

The operation section or volume may be the largest one by far in some cases, as in many user manuals for software, where description, installation, and maintenance are subjects requiring relatively little documentation, while operation is the most discursive subject and dominates the user instructions. (Software maintenance, for example, is a subject with much greater application to mainframe computer programs than to personal computer programs. Even then it is not a subject of interest or utility to the typical user and so is rarely even referred to in the typical user manual for software programs.) The opposite situation may prevail in many cases, such as manuals for complex systems that are relatively simple to operate, but require a great deal of service—preventive maintenance—and fairly complex corrective and O&R maintenance.

In the case of the program for management of an investment portfolio, for example, instructions for operation represent approximately one half of the entire manual, with no coverage of maintenance.

In the case of some other programs, especially those that by their nature require rather little in description and installation information, the preponderance of operating-information coverage is even more apparent. The 54-page O'Neill Software *Electra-Find* manual, for example, devotes only two pages to description and three pages to installation, with the remaining 49 pages devoted to operating instructions.

The *Operator's Manual* for the North Atlantic Qantex 7030/7040 printer (introduced earlier) offers an interesting example. It devotes three pages to description, 18 pages to installation, and 10 pages to operation. However, the remaining 42 pages of information furnish general technical data that may be used for any purpose, and there are 43 illustrations and 55 tables that are available as general reference information for any purpose.

Whirlpool's *Use & Care Guide* for its latest model dishwasher devotes virtually the entire user instructions—15 pages—to operating guidance, obviously not expecting the user to be interested in, or have use for, maintenance instructions, other than those cautionary notes that are a normal part of operating instructions.

MAINTENANCE

When the product is a consumer product—a product normally purchased and used by the lay consumer—little maintenance instruction is included in the user's manual, and the information that is there will rarely be very technical. This is not to say that the user may not in some cases be an expert—some of the hobbyists and aficionados are more expert than the professionals of the field—but it is assumed that the average or typical buyer of a consumer product is a lay person and not interested in becoming a technical expert. There are generally, therefore, two levels of maintenance documentation for users: that for the typical consumer, as nontechnical as possible, and that for the professional, with technical detail. Equipment, from automobiles to toasters, is backed with technical data documented principally for maintenance purposes and principally for professionals in maintenance. Even software producers often offer "source" documents, which contain technical details not furnished in the general user documentation. (In most cases this is special data, available at extra cost, distinct from those manuals or other instructions included in the original package.)

A 21-page manual for assembling a Kent International bicycle comes labeled both *Bicycle Assembly* and *Maintenance Manual* on its cover. In fact, only five pages are actually devoted to maintenance instruction, including a trouble symptom/diagnostics chart, a service parts list, and a set of maintenance procedures. Most of the rest of it is devoted to assembly instructions.

When it comes to the military, maintenance data and documentation assume an importance all their own for reasons that include both the urgency of operational dependability under tactical conditions and the rigorous conditions under which military equipment must operate in the field. In short, the military cannot afford to risk equipment failure, especially of equipment used tactically in the field, no matter the cost to minimize the risk. Therefore, with only rare exception, the military imposes requirements for maintenance documentation for greater than that demanded in other markets and by other users.

Still another common requirement of the military, although not uncommon in commercial applications, is the illustrated parts breakdown ("IPB," in the parlance). This is built on the concept of exploded-view drawings, showing graphically how the equipment or portion of the equipment is assembled and/or may be disassembled. This is quite a useful idea for commercial user manuals too, and is used, usually in somewhat more simplified and less costly form, as shown in Figure 3–7. In this case each numbered part is identified in a separate list, using the number for reference. In other cases the parts may be identified by lettering on the drawing itself.

The military agencies have also developed, over the years, many standards and specifications for commonly used parts and components of electronic, aeronautical, naval, mechanical, and other classes of equipment and supplies. They often require that whenever a military standard or specification exists for a component, the component must conform to the standard or specification.

Much the same consideration applies to the documents themselves. The military organizations have developed many standards and specifications for documents of various kinds. These prescribe abbreviations, drawing practices, symbols to be used in schematic drawings, kinds of information required, and numerous other details governing the documentation.

None of these are automatically applied to military documentation. The contract specifies which standards and specifications are to apply. This may depend on any of several factors, such as the budget available, because sometimes the customer simply cannot afford the documentation he or she would prefer. (Some of these kinds of documentation are quite costly.) But other factors also enter into the matter. The documentation needs of equipment destined for use in the field are evaluated differently than are those for equipment to be used in a local headquarters establishment, and requirements for equipment destined for use in jungles are different than those for equipment to be used in deserts.

FIGURE 3–7 An Exploded View of a Bicycle and Its Parts List

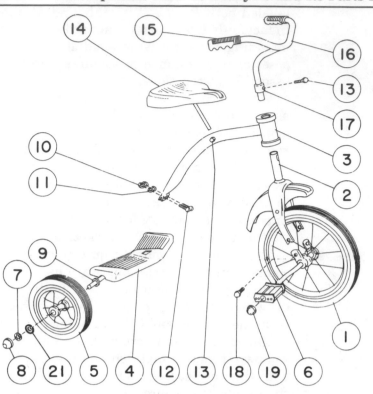

PARTS LIST

NO.	PART NAME	NO. REQ'D.	ORDERING NO.	PRICE EACH
1	Pedal Wheel 10'' (254 mm)	1	09-0305E	
2	Fork & Fender Assembly	1	701	
3	Backbone Assembly	1	01-0521	
4	Rear Deck Assembly	1	01-0250	
5	Rear Wheel 7'' (117.8 mm)	2	08-0320E	
6	Pedal	2	KK-0001	
7	Pushnut Fastener	2	HH-0196	
8	Hub Cap	2	MM-0290	
9	3/4 x 25/64 x 18 ga. Washer (19.0 x 9.9 x 1.2 mm)	2	HH-0983	
10	1/4 Hex. Nut (6.3 mm)	2	HH-0427	
11	1/4 Lockwasher (6.3 mm)	2	HH-1002	
12	1/4-20 x 7/8'' Round Head Bolt (6.3 x 22.2 mm)	2	HH-0658	
13	Set Screw	2	HH-0778	
14	Seat	1	07-0070	
15	Handlebar Grip	2	JJ -0058	
16	Handlebar	1	02-0139	
17	Locking Collar	1	03-0100	
18	5/16-24 x 1/2'' Hex. Hd. Bolt (7.9 x 12.7 mm)	2	HH-0627	
19	7/16 United Carr Cap (11.1mm)	2	HH-0198	
20	10'' Fender Decals (254 mm)	1	FF-1153	
21	Hub Cap Washer	2	58-0016	

MAINTENANCE PHILOSOPHY

Prescribed maintenance procedures are the product of a maintenance philosophy or concept of how maintenance should be approached. And that, in turn, depends on (1) user needs and conditions, and (2) equipment characteristics (which are themselves the result of the engineering design philosophy). For example, maintenance documentation for electronic equipment has changed greatly in recent years, as the vacuum tube has passed to almost total nonexistence under the rapid development of solid-state electronics into today's increasingly miniaturized circuits mounted on chips. Maintenance of electronic equipment no longer consists of measuring and troubleshooting circuits down to the replacement of a single resistor or capacitor. To a large degree electronic maintenance has become chip diagnostics and replacement, and even board diagnostics and replacement, in many cases.

The practicality of today's costs—the high cost of labor, principally— has had its effect also, and in a great many cases maintenance consists of simple replacement of major components or subassemblies, if not total replacement of the end item! The cost of an entire curcuit board is often far less than the cost of the labor necessary to identify and replace a single defective chip on the board. But that is not confined to electronics equipment alone: Chips and chip technology have invaded numerous other fields and are found in use in many other kinds of equipment, and the design/maintenance philosophies based on complete assemblies and subassemblies is apparent in many fields. For example, the daisy wheel printer and the solenoid assembly that provides the motive force are each replaceable, but in the typical dot matrix printer the entire printhead is a single unit that is discarded and easily replaced with a new one in normal maintenance. In fact, a trend to designing modern equipment as a configuration of replaceable major units is in evidence, perhaps driven by the high cost of labor for maintenance and by modern thinking in system terms, but certainly influenced also by the high cost of labor in manufacturing processes.

For the military there is an additional consideration in the philosophy of maintenance via replacement of major components and assemblies: This maintenance approach is usually the fastest means to restoring operation of anything that has failed functionally, a consideration that can make a major difference under tactical conditions. And for such reasons as this the military has established echelons of maintenance, with the first level by the operators and/or local technicians, doing both preventive maintenance (prescribed periodic inspections, cleaning, lubrication, and replacement of worn or otherwise suspect items) and corrective maintenance via total replacement of assemblies or subassemblies with spare units. A second level of maintenance involves taking the equipment/system off-line to troubleshoot problems and perform repairs. The third level is "depot maintenance," which entails sending the equipment off to some central point for total overhaul.

In some cases, particularly in complex and critically important systems, maintenance provisions are built into the equipment as various controls and indicators that identify problems. Some even have backup or redundant subsystems that are automatically switched in when a primary system fails.

The considerations discussed in this chapter have been primarily those of the manufacturers of the products and the writers of the documentation. In the next chapter we will begin to consider the needs and problems of the users—those who read the documentation.

The Problems of Writers, Readers, and Managers

If the authors of user instructions are inexperienced writers, readers are often equally inexperienced users. Documentation managers also have problems.

THE INEXPERIENCED WRITER

One of the major and most common faults of inexperienced writers is an inability to write to anyone other than their peers. When the expert artisan who designed a magnificent glass and metal etagere is assigned the task of writing assembly instructions he or she tends to prepare instructions suitable for a peer—someone with equivalent skills. This often takes the form of a rough sketch, a list of parts, and a list of procedures detailing the order of assembly, all within a page or two, and with a brief mention of the tools required. Any other artisan or handy individual should be able to assemble the etagere from those instructions with no trouble at all.

But the root problem is not that simple; there are a number of other complicating factors.

THE INEXPERIENCED USER

Unfortunately, many, if not most, of the readers of instructions are not artisans, engineers, mechanics, or even handy. They do not know the difference between a sheet metal screw, a self-tapping screw, a wood screw, or stove bolt, much less recognize a lag bolt, a pan head screw, a finishing nail, or a key wrench. They are, in fact, often quite surprised and sometimes even outraged to discover that anyone has assumed that they do or should know such things.

AN EXAMPLE

A set of assembly instructions for a child's crib manufactured by an Indiana firm is offered on the two sides of a 5 by 8 inch sheet of paper, with three photographs. The dominant photograph occupies more than one half of the first side and illustrates the 40 items to be found in the hardware bag. The text begins with an instruction to "remove the two stabilizer bars wired to the bed spring," but those bars are identified in a faded and barely legible photograph on the other side of the sheet. The text goes on to instruct the user to install the stabilizer bars, but with no guidance at all as to where they fit, other than on "headboard and footboard." Parenthetically, at this point, *after the instruction to install the stabilizer bars* (apparently an afterthought of the author of those instructions), the text digresses abruptly and instructs the reader to also remove the "four metal crib rods for later use" while removing the stabilizer rods.

These instructions may be less cryptic when the reader is actually observing the unassembled crib, if the reader has experience and/or some knack or instinct for mechanical work. But even that individual will find the instructions unclear. There are, in fact, several specific faults in this instruction sheet.

First, the photographs are of poor quality. They should either be of far better quality or the writer should have line drawings made. The latter would probably have been an improvement because even good quality photographs often fail to show necessary details.

Second, the text is muddy. Obviously it was not reviewed and rewritten or the author would have realized that his opening paragraph was badly organized and presented instructions in illogical order and without true how-to guidance. (It gets even worse in subsequent paragraphs.)

Finally, the decision to confine the instructions to a single small sheet was a bad one. Even with excessively condensed instructions, it was necessary to use very small type to squeeze it all onto such a small sheet. (I have seen more space given to instructions for setting a digital clock!)

INEXPERIENCED READERS

There is another factor to consider: If many skilled engineers, designers, and other professionals are unskilled writers, many capable users are unskilled readers. That is, the user who is perfectly comfortable with tools and equipment is often equally uncomfortable with words, and so may have almost as much difficulty comprehending and using printed instruction as the mechanically inept user.

This is not really a matter of literacy as much as it is a matter of human tendencies to favor the easy and convenient. Unfortunately, even highly educated individuals in our society are often poor readers because the comfortable reading level of many, even of college graduates, is rated at eighth to tenth grade, the average to be found in most newspapers and popular magazines. Many can read more difficult prose, with additional effort, but tend to resist the discomfort of the extra effort if the material is not of extreme importance to them. *Reader's Digest* is often cited as an example of lucid writing at this approximate level and the distinctive style of that periodical has become a de facto standard for many other publications.

On the other hand, some devices require little instruction because they are completely assembled or nearly so, they are quite simple devices, and/or they are so well illustrated with photographs or drawings that little text need be added. See Figure 4–1 for a good example of this. (The figure itself is more of a sketch than a finished drawing—it appears to have been sketched via a simple dot matrix printer—but it serves the purpose well because the equipment is simple and comes assembled, although it has several removable and adjustable parts.) There is a second sheet bearing the operating instructions (see Figure 4–2) that covers all the procedures and contingencies, including an explanation of a new type of roller being used in a simplified design, replacing an older style felt-covered roller. (This explanation is for the benefit of anyone familiar with the company's older models.)

Note the simple and straightforward language used in the two sheets, offering clear instructions for all recommended procedures. Note also the judicious use of drawings—three are used to illustrate what is a relatively small and simple machine—for whatever the reader must be able to *visualize*. First there is the main drawing that shows how the ribbon is positioned in this model MacInker. (There are several different models for different types of ribbons, with appropriate drawings, of course.) Then there are separate drawings for the two components that are adjustable, the ribbon guide and the inking roller.

THE RELUCTANCE FACTOR

The sardonic jest that "when all else fails read the instructions" is more than humor: it reflects a modern truth. Many people are increasingly reluctant to read at all. Perhaps it is the influence of TV, but we seem to have become much more a society of watchers—viewers—than of readers. We would much rather look at pictures than read words. The average user will look at, even study, photographs and drawings, but is likely to forgo reading the textual instructions until and unless he or she is in serious difficulties and looking almost desperately for help.

The military have recognized this too, and have experimented widely with soldiers' manuals created as cartoon booklets on such basic military subjects as disassembly, cleaning, and reassembly of personal weapons. Reading ability—or the lack of it—is a problem in spite of

FIGURE 4–1 Assembly and Operation of MacInker

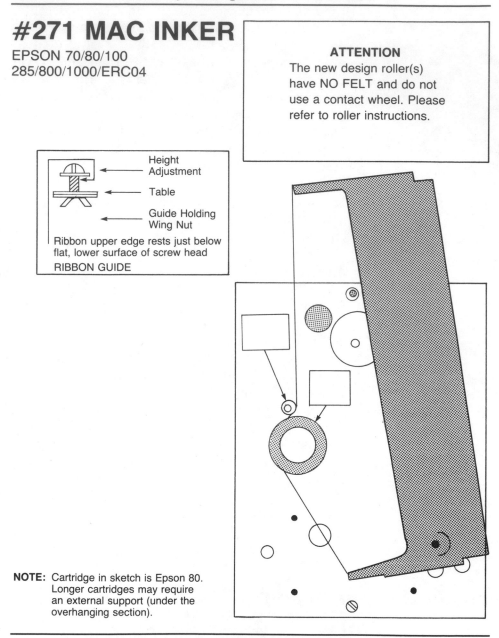

#271 MAC INKER

EPSON 70/80/100
285/800/1000/ERC04

ATTENTION
The new design roller(s)
have NO FELT and do not
use a contact wheel. Please
refer to roller instructions.

Height Adjustment

Table

Guide Holding Wing Nut

Ribbon upper edge rests just below flat, lower surface of screw head

RIBBON GUIDE

NOTE: Cartridge in sketch is Epson 80. Longer cartridges may require an external support (under the overhanging section).

Courtesy of Computer Friends, Inc.

the requirement of a high school diploma as a requisite for induction into the armed forces. To at least some degree, therefore, the comic-book approach to the military training manuals that most soldiers find dreadfully dull has helped.

That is not the only evidence of the need for better presentation techniques of what is usually uninteresting subject matter; other experience has demonstrated clearly that the ability to read text well is linked closely to motivation. In Job Corps centers, for example, the reading ability of those judged functionally illiterate proved to be variable, rather than absolute. Corpsmembers' reading ability—functional

FIGURE 4–2 Procedural Instructions for MacInker

#504 NEW DESIGN ROLLER , NON ROTATING, FELTLESS

The new, non-rotating, feltless roller design can be used (in most cases) in older style MAC INKER(s) by removing the aluminum post nearer to the cartridge, and with most universal and new, dedicated MAC INKER(s).

Place the 504 reservoir in the same location as used by the other types of reservoirs (501 - 503). The reservoir mounts with a wing-nut. Do not overtighten, as the reservoir may need to be rotated to adjust the aperture location.

Note that the Contact Wheel is not needed, but it can be used, if so desired. In the new kits with this type of reservoir, the Contact Wheel will not be included.

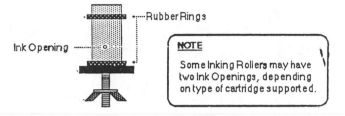

#504 - NEW DESIGN, NON-ROTATING, FELTLESS ROLLER

1) Route the ribbon in the same way as shown in the applicable MAC INKER cartridge drawing.

2) Adjust the 2 'O' rings so that the ribbon is centered over the ink aperture. The aperture is located directly under the Index Mark, on top of the reservoir.

3) Rotate the reservoir so that the aperture is covered by the ribbon.

4) Start the motor and add some ink to the reservoir, half reservoir or less, particularly during first time operation. Remember that the shorter the ribbon length, the less ink will be required.

5) The ink will be applied in a strip approximately 1/8" wide. If a heavier application is desired, turn the reservoir toward the direction where the ribbon comes out of the cartridge. When the aperture is partly uncovered a bubble of ink will form, float and eventually be applied to the ribbon.

VERY IMPORTANT
When re-inking is completed, **remove promptly all residual ink from the reservoir,** as there is no felt to absorb the left-over ink. Create a small vacuum by pressing the body of the bottle (nozzle up please!!) and insert the nozzle into the reservoir. Release the pressure on the body of the bottle. The ink wil be re-absorbed inside.
Should the ink aperture become clogged **DO NOT USE A PAPER CLIP** to remove the blockage. **Use a pin or thin needle.**

literacy, that is—increased sharply under certain conditions. Most, for example, read comic books with relative ease and facility, as compared with their abilities to read straight narrative texts. There are several significant influences on reading ability, such as these:

Comfort factor.
Long-term benefit.
Short-term benefit.

THE COMFORT FACTOR

The comfort factor is the inverse of the reluctance factor. Under most circumstances an individual is far more likely to read text that *appears* to be easy to read—text with large type, short sentences, short paragraphs, and lots of white space—as compared with the formidable appearance of lengthy blocks of solid text in small type. This is a pure case of the comfort factor versus the reluctance factor: It helps when you can somehow *lure* the reader into reading with a distinct and deliberate *effort* to understand by making reading and understanding of the material appear easy, if not rewarding in itself.

The most relevant short-term or immediate benefit of reading is *enjoyment*. This refers to the ability of the material to somehow capture the reader's interest by providing a promise or clearly implied promise of an immediately entertaining, useful, or curiosity-satisfying experience.

LONG-TERM BENEFIT

Long-term benefits, such as a diploma or a career after three or four years' effort, rarely work with individuals who are basically unmotivated, and that applies equally to the motivation of readers. It applies especially in the case of reading user instructions, which are usually not a particularly important matter to the subject at best. Moreover, the promise of a long-term benefit, however framed and presented, is almost inevitably an *extrinsic* factor, a consideration we will look at again in a moment.

SHORT-TERM BENEFIT

The idea of reward or short-term benefit as a motivator is widely accepted, but often misunderstood and, even worse, misapplied. Experiments have been conducted in which the subjects were rewarded with money, for example, to induce them to work harder at improving their reading skills. However, other experiments have shown rather clearly that the short-term benefit is far more effective when it is *intrinsic,* rather than extrinsic. A reward of money for reading well is extrinsic, for example; it is offered in the hope that it will induce the subject to do something the subject may very well (and probably does) find somewhat distasteful or a reward would not be necessary. On the other hand, a truly intrinsic benefit is a reward that results directly from the act of reading. If reading can be made pleasurable in itself—its own reward—no further reward is needed, of course.

Obviously, user instructions can never offer readers the pleasure they might get from an interesting novel or magazine article, but an improvement in the writing of instructions can be made by pursuing at least three approaches to help the reader:

- Maximize the comfort factor.
- Utilize all "easy reading" principles possible.
- Borrow some of the writing techniques used in developing fiction and popular nonfiction.

MAXIMIZING THE COMFORT FACTOR

Actually, the comfort factor should be considered as two phases in reading: (1) the contemplation of the material and the anticipation of reading it—the impression it makes on the reader as to its probable difficulty; and (2) the actual reading experience, which is really covered under the second item listed above. The easy reading principles of such authorities as Dr. Rudolph Flesch are guidelines for maximizing reading comfort through reducing the strain to grasp meaning and an inferred sense of inadequacy as a result of that condition.

Appearance as a Comfort Factor

The appearance of being easy to read is a result of the physical layout of the instructions as presented. The most basic favorable influences result from these practices and characteristics:

- An "open" appearance: Not more than six lines to the inch (vertically), generous paragraph indents, extra space ("leading") between paragraphs, and generous use of white space generally.
- Free and frequent use of free-standing headlines and blurbs or glosses, set in distinctive typefaces, such as bold or italic, using common and easily understood words.
- Body-type size not smaller than 10 point.
- Generous use of illustrations, preferably simple line drawings, but uncomplicated photographs, if photographs are used.
- "Callouts" (identifying labels) on illustrations. (See Figure 4–3 for example of callouts.)

Actual Reading Comfort

The most common advice offered for writing easy-to-read material is that of confining your writing to short words, short or simple sentences, and uncomplicated grammatical structures. But that is unfortunately too much like the formula for business success to "find a need and fill it" and that for stock market success to "buy low and sell high." It's advice incontestable in principle only, describing an ideal, without giving the faintest clue as to the means for achieving that ideal, or even truly defining the means. Who can say what is a short word and what is a simple sentence. The problem and the solution—readability mea-

FIGURE 4–3   Line Drawings Using Callouts

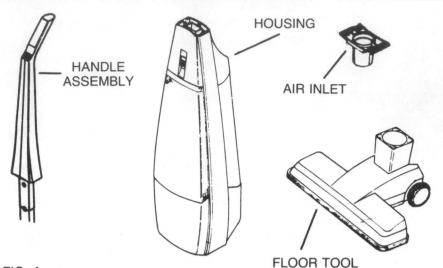

HOUSING

HANDLE
ASSEMBLY

AIR INLET

FLOOR TOOL

FIG. A

— There are 6 screws in the fastener package. The three different type screws and their uses are described below (fig. B)

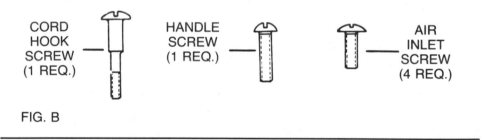

CORD
HOOK
SCREW
(1 REQ.)

HANDLE
SCREW
(1 REQ.)

AIR
INLET
SCREW
(4 REQ.)

FIG. B

sures and formulas—are far more complicated than that. These measures have to do with vocabularies, too, perhaps more than with any other factor. And that is not a simple matter.

For one thing, everyone has at least two vocabularies, a speaking vocabulary and a reading vocabulary. The first is probably the smallest for most of us, and the latter the largest. I suspect that most of us, even professional writers, have a writing vocabulary that falls between the first two in size.

There is no doubt that we all read and manage to grasp at least the broad meanings of many words that we do not know well enough to use in conversation. That is partly because we can infer the meanings of many unfamiliar words we read, either because their context suggests their meanings or the author has used some device to assist the reader in grasping the meanings. In fact, most of us owe a large part of our individual vocabularies to words we have added in this manner, through reading and inferring their meanings.

READABILITY VERSUS UNDERSTANDABILITY

What the foregoing means, significantly, is that a reader need not necessarily know in advance all the words a writer uses. The motivated reader can infer the meanings of strange words, especially if the writer anticipates the reader's possible difficulty and provides a bit of assistance, such as a parenthetical remark that defines or elaborates on the word. Helping the reader in this way makes the copy far easier to understand, although the effect will not show up in readability measures. In fact, many of the measures you can apply to make printed instructions far more easily understandable will not be reflected in readability measures. This is because these measures are applied primarily to the words used, which may, in an absolute sense, measure something called *readability*. However, readability does not equate with *understandability,* which is far more to the point here. Readability is only one facet of understandability, and in many cases—notably cases such as those under discussion here—readability alone is not nearly enough.

Following are a few characteristics of well-designed and well-executed—highly understandable—instructional materials:

- Definitions or help in understanding, supplied by one means or another, for all terms and words likely to be unknown to the reader.
- Consistency in nomenclature. For example, a part called a *retainer spring* introduced as a retainer spring is always a retainer spring. Don't call it a pressure spring in another place, unless you explain the change of name carefully and completely. But don't do it at all if it can be avoided.
- Unambiguous statements. It is necessary to edit carefully for possible ambiguities by estimating whether a given statement *could* be reasonably misinterpreted to mean anything other than the author's intended meaning.
- Consistency in presenting procedural instructions in the order in which they are to be performed.
- Analogies, similes, and other imagery to help translate the unfamiliar into familiar contexts.
- Tables and matrices to help readers understand concepts, contrasts, comparisons, commonalities, and/or relationships discussed.
- Examples used freely. This is particularly important. Many readers are able to cite what they read and so appear to have learned. But the real test of learning is the ability to *apply* the instructions. Many people cannot do this without first seeing specific examples of applications.
- Many drawings, even simple line drawings or sketches, to illustrate the parts, ideas, procedures, and other items.
- Callouts in drawings and photographs, preferably directly on the drawing or photograph, of all items referred to in text.
- Exploded views to show order of assembly or disassembly.

HOW TO WRITE VERSUS WHAT TO WRITE

We are getting a bit ahead of ourselves in delving into these matters now. My experience as a writer, editor, and manager has shown me that for many writers the struggle is not a problem in *how* to write as much as in *what* to write. When they do not know precisely what they ought to present to readers, they flounder about in search of ideas rather than in search of words. Yet, they manage to deceive themselves about the nature of their writing problem. They do not want to admit, even to themselves, that they do not know what to say about the fields in which they are experts. So they deceive themselves into believing that they simply do not know how to write well—that has become an acceptable frailty today! Because of such problems as this, engineers assigned to write instructions for maintenance technicians offer a great deal of unnecessary and even irrelevant data: they tend to write to peers, writing about the subject an engineer knows best—engineering—which seems to them to be rational enough under the circumstances.

Knowing the engineer's design rationale may or may not be relevant to the maintenance tasks (although it usually is not), but certainly most of the engineering history is of no use. In fact, even circuit theory below the level of subassembly is less and less relevant in these times. Today, maintenance has become more a matter of diagnosis, down to the replacement of entire subassemblies ("throwaway" parts). Knowledge of how individual circuits work is less and less relevant to maintenance.

Still, that is not an absolute either. "Line" maintenance—aboard a ship at sea, for example—may involve identifying a failed subassembly and its replacement, but depot maintenance may involve overhaul and repair of the subassembly for use again. That is only one example, for maintenance of major systems is usually conducted at a minimum of three levels:

Preventive.
Corrective.
Overhaul and repair.

The writing of instructions for each level is quite different from that for the other two levels. It is generally dictated by the nature of what must be done at each level, what tools and equipment are required at each level, and what technician's qualifications—skills and knowledge—are required at each level.

Let's consider each of these factors briefly, continuing to use maintenance instruction for this example. (Remember, however, that the same philosophy will apply to other types of user instructions.)

What Must Be Done at Each Level

The writer—assuming that he or she is also responsible for specifying the maintenance procedures, a usual requirement—must first decide what the maintenance *philosophy* is to be. For example, will there be *preventive* maintenance? (It is desirable, but not always a practicable approach.) Will there be *corrective* maintenance? (Probably so; it is by far the most common kind of maintenance.) Will there be *depot maintenance?* (That depends largely on the nature of the equipment, as does the question of preventive maintenance.) For our purposes here, let us assume that there will be maintenance at all three levels and that there will be a single maintenance manual with separate sections for each level. Other questions also arise in establishing a maintenance philosophy, such as what kinds of maintenance operations are to be conducted at each level (ergo, what spare parts are needed at each level).

Once the basic maintenance philosophy is clarified, preparations for writing can begin. Those preparations should include the development of a definitive outline, and this is where many writers run into problems. Too often the outline assumes a shape such as this:

I. Maintenance.
   A. Preventive.
      1. Inspections.
      2. Lubrication.
   B. Corrective.
      1. Troubleshooting.
      2. Diagnosis.
      3. Replacement.
   C. Overhaul and repair.
      1. Disassembly.
      2. Inspection.
      3. Replacement of parts.
      4. Reassembly.

That may appear to the untrained eye to be a good outline. In fact it is the kind of outline that leads to trouble for at least two reasons: (1) the writer has not made other than general and vague commitments; and (2) the editor and/or manager reviewing the manuscript has no way of judging how well the writer has carried out the task.

In fact, the outline shown must be carried at least one step further, preferably several steps further, as in this example:

I. Maintenance.
   A. Preventive.
      1. Tools, materials, and equipment required.
      2. Procedures.
         a. Inspections.
            (1) All moving parts for wear, play, fit.
            (2) All belts and pulleys for wear, estimated useful life remaining.
            (3) Lights, dials, gauges, other indicators.
         b. Lubrication.
            (1) Gears and bearings.
            (2) Levers and other moving parts.
         c. Measurements.
            (1) Meter readings.
            (2) Slack in belts and pulleys.

In a given case the outline should go at least one step further—down to one additional level of detail, that is—as appropriate to the specific equipment or system, identifying specific items of the equipment. And the outline would be carried on to other sections of the manual and other subjects at the same level of detail.

Overall, the idea is to plan the writing in detail before beginning, trying to anticipate all needs and problems. But the plans must also provide to those who must review and approve the manuscripts (especially in their final versions) enough detail to enable them to judge two things: (1) the adequacy of the "book plan" beforehand; and (2) the adequacy of the execution.

Perhaps the most direct way to express the idea is this: It is not enough to describe in your outline what you will write *about;* you must describe what you will *say* in your manuscript. If you study the two outline samples shown here, the meaning of that should become plain. Anyone can generalize about most things; it is the ability to provide details that proves expert knowledge—even to yourself, as the writer.

ESSENTIAL FOR BOTH WRITERS AND MANAGERS

To produce an outline of this type and at this level of detail, tying it firmly to the specific equipment, requires that the writer know the subject and the equipment thoroughly. That is the main objective of requiring this kind of outline: it is the proof that the writer does know the subject and has done adequate research or otherwise acquired the requisite knowledge. It also provides assurance of adequate planning. If you are a writer you ought to demand of yourself such detailed planning and preparation as personal proof of your own readiness to begin serious writing. It is amazingly easy to deceive yourself—to convince yourself that you know your subject well enough to write about it when, in truth, you do not. It is a necessary self-discipline. The first time you attempt to produce such an outline as part of your detailed planning and you find that you cannot do so without further research and contemplation, you will find it a shocking experience. But it is an unforgettable one, a valuable education, even a revelation.

If you are a supervisor or manager of documentation programs you can have even more shocking and costly experiences. These often demonstrate rather dramatically why such detailed plans must be made and presented as proof that the writer is prepared to do the job properly. A few horror stories drawn from past debacles will illustrate why this is an absolute essential.

A young technical writer working on the documentation of a new Navy shipboard missile system (the ill-fated TYPHON system) spent the better part of a year making notes of his research. This included studies of other documentation, interviews, field trips, and other energetic activity. He was counseled by older, more experienced writers to start converting his growing pile of notes into a rough-draft manuscript or, at least, a detailed outline. He insisted, however, that he would do so as soon as his note-taking was complete or nearly so. Unfortunately, by that time he had forgotten the significance of many of his notes and could not even decipher many of them.

Similar, but even more disastrous was the case of a technician assigned as a technical writer to the huge BMEWS (Ballistic Missile Early Warning System) project at RCA Service Company in New Jersey. This technical writer collected notes voluminously over an 18-month period. When required to surrender his rough-draft manuscript for editing he resigned and left the company. He left nothing behind but a notebook full of scrawled and largely cryptic notes and a large hole in the BMEWS documentation program.

In the case of a technical writing project for the NASA Goddard Space Flight Center a technical writer bent over his desk in a secluded corner all day every day for almost a year, even during many overtime hours for which he claimed a need. But one day, suddenly aroused to misgivings about this individual's technical knowledge by something he had overheard the man say, the general manager demanded to see at least some of his draft. It was then finally revealed that he had not even written notes, and had absolutely nothing to show for all the hours and dollars he had dissipated.

These may appear to be exaggerated cases of mismanagement or, perhaps more to the point, lack of management, but such incidents are too numerous to be dismissed as aberrations. Writing is subject to just these problems because of its nature, and such rigid discipline as that suggested here is necessary to establish and maintain firm control.

There is at least one other important advantage in having such outlines developed: They are an excellent and virtually indispensable tool for getting help from technical experts and management in the planning stages. Given the generalized, "topical outlines" shown earlier, managers and technical experts can hardly do much but approve, and are unlikely to make much contribution. Give them details, however, and they will both critique the plans and make helpful comments and suggestions. This is borne out by experience: the more detailed are the initial plans presented, the more detailed are the comments, criticisms, suggestions, and contributions made by all who are asked to review and contribute at any and all stages of the effort.

This is equally true of plans submitted to the customer for review and approval (even when the customer is another department or division of your own corporation), and perhaps even more significantly as an aid in getting the project approved and completed efficiently.

THE RESEARCH PLAN

Just as the final product must be planned, so should the effort overall be planned. That means establishing a research plan, among other things (such as schedules and assignments). Research can take many forms and pursue many avenues, including any or all of the following:

- Applicable standards and specifications.
- Other documents (library research).

- Interviews.
- Direct observation.
- Personal knowledge.

Applicable Standards and Specifications

Generally this applies to manuals prepared for the military and, to some and usually much more limited extent, other government agencies and/or large organizations. Military organizations have well developed standards and specifications for their documents, and these are usually a first order of priority. However, many other large organizations, both government and private, have documentation standards and specifications of their own. The Government Printing Office has a manual of style, for example, that sets forth its requirements; that manual has been adopted by others and is often invoked as a standard. There are also several other style manuals in popular use, and many organizations have developed their own style guides. If there is one applicable to your own effort, it usually becomes a high-priority requirement.

Library Research

There are many other documents that are of use in developing user instructions, including some or all of these:

- Laboratory logs.
- Original proposals.
- Reports.
- Engineering notes and sketches.
- Formal engineering drawings.
- User instructions on earlier and similar end-items.
- Competitors' user instructions on similar end-items.

Interviews

In many projects, especially those involving technical products and lengthy developmental phases, the writer must talk with the designers and developers, spending time reviewing the product and asking the designers to suggest coverage and supply specific information. This is often a relatively difficult task, however, and it is a good idea to use this kind of last resort when you have exhausted all other avenues for reliable information. The busy engineer is likely to become quite impatient at being asked questions to which the correct answers are fairly obvious or easily obtained elsewhere. (This is a basic rule for all interviewing: prepare by using all normal avenues for information and confine your interview to questions where the answers are not easily obtainable elsewhere.)

Direct Observation

It is often necessary to simply observe the items at first hand, to examine them, to witness their operation, to operate them yourself, sometimes even to assemble or disassemble them personally to verify drawings and other raw source data. In any case, such observation is most helpful in lending you confidence in what you write or cause to have written.

Personal Knowledge

Your own knowledge is a decided high-priority asset and resource. Use your personal knowledge of any technologies involved, history of similar projects, and/or other relevant matters. However, personal knowledge is most useful (and most often useful) in combination with the other methods and resources, as a means for digesting, analyzing, and interpreting information gained via the other sources and resources.

EMPATHY

Perhaps the most valuable asset a writer can have, and among the most difficult to acquire is *empathy*. That is the ability to see things through the reader's eyes. Many writers have that ability without consciously working to acquire it. I believe it can be acquired with distinct effort. The effort consists of continuous practice in examining and analyzing your drafts to detect ambiguities, anomalies, and other potential pitfalls for the reader. Put yourself in the reader's place—what do you want to know? What do you *need* to know to get the job done? The most effective writers, especially the "how-to" genre of writers, have that gift.

However, empathy is not extrasensory perception; you do not depend on divine inspiration for it. Empathy is rooted in highly practical considerations. It requires that you have an advance understanding and definition of your reader.

DEFINITION OF THE READER: A PREREQUISITE

Identifying and defining your reader is a necessary prerequisite for empathy. But empathy begins to play its role long before writing begins. It is a prerequisite to all planning, and is the first or nearly the first consideration in planning. You may very well have several readers, each with different characteristics—especially when you are producing a set of manuals, each designed for a different purpose.

Characteristics to Be Defined

There are two broad areas to consider in identifying and defining readers before you do serious planning:

1. What the reader is to do with the information you are to supply—
   what *use* he or she is to make of it.
2. What level of relevant knowledge he or she has before reading the
   instructions you are to provide.

These two items probably appear far simpler than they are. Each
requires substantial amplification.

Why the information is required

In fact we have covered this ground earlier and need only to recap
briefly here. In most cases the information you provide is needed to
carry out one or more of the following tasks:

Assembly.
Installation.
Operation.
Preventive maintenance.
Corrective maintenance.
Overhaul and repair.
Management.

We have not considered management before, but often user instructions are intended for managers who will not be involved directly in
any of these listed tasks, but who must understand the equipment or
system to discharge their management responsibilities. Some of the
coverage in military manuals for large systems is intended for officers
at junior, field, and/or general rank because they are the responsible
managers.

Qualifications of the reader

It is an essential that you have a good understanding of the reader's
qualifications for carrying out the intended tasks. On the one hand you
must understand your text and put it to use effectively. But it is equally
impractical to deliver information so basic to the reader that it is a
waste of time to read your instructions.

This is where so many technical writers err. Military documentation
standards and specifications are usually heavily detailed—some think
too much so—because it is hoped that they will guide the writer well
in creating exactly the right product, and they are a great help indeed.
But they are not a complete cure for the problem. Too many writers
still address their peers, either unable to understand that their readers
are less knowledgeable than they or unable to develop the necessary
empathy. I have personally heard writers remonstrating with the technical experts who represent their resources and reviewers that more
detail is needed, only to hear the experts snort, "Oh, the reader will
know that!" (After hearing that rejoinder a number of times there is
an almost irresistible temptation to inquire as to why the book is necessary at all!)

How Much Detail Does the Reader Need?

It is far better to err in providing excessive detail than in providing insufficient detail, much as it is to be preferred that the level of detail be just right. While we try to define the knowledge or skill level of a typical or average reader, there really is no typical or average reader: the knowledge and skills of the readers vary over a rather wide range. So we usually wind up writing to the estimated least knowledgeable and least skilled reader, despite the reader definition supplied us as basic input information (or developed by us, as the case may be).

In the case of user instructions for the general consumer, for example, we must assume that the reader does not know a toggle bolt from an egg slicer. We will be wrong about that for some percentage of the buyers who do happen to have good skills and experience in relevant areas and are completely at ease as they read our instructions for assembly, adjustment, and installation of our company's patented home exerciser. If you assume that men are more apt than women at reading and using user instructions you are in the wrong pew; in more than a few households it is the woman of the house, not the man, who manages to assemble the combination spice rack and vegetable shredder and get it all tuned up and working properly after dear old dad has been forced to give up on it.

USER INSTRUCTIONS AS TRAINING

While user instructions vary enormously in all respects, writing them is still of the writing-to-inform class. In many cases the technical manuals we are called on to prepare are to be used as the textbooks for training programs. This is particularly true for many military programs. In a greater sense all user instructions are training materials, especially when the instructions must train the householder in tenons and mortises or other strange lore as a preliminary to following the assembly instructions. Bearing this in mind—that the user instructions are training materials—is helpful in judging what information is needed and how much detail is likely to be most useful.

WRITING STYLES AND FORMATS

Writing to inform requires that the information be presented in a logical or progressive pattern. A novelist, or even a writer of popular nonfiction, may experiment with flashbacks and other devices. But unorthodox presentations are usually totally unsuited to how-to writing. Probably the best sequence of presentation is the time-honored one: from the general to the particular, when functional theory or philosophy is being taught, and "cookbook" style—almost "take screwdriver in left hand"—when specific procedures are to be taught.

One manual for MS-DOS, the operating system for my computer, introduces the FORMAT command thus:

Format
Purpose: The FORMAT command prepares disks to store MS-DOS files. Disks must be formatted before they can be used by MS-DOS.

Another manual for MS-DOS introduces the command thus:

The Format Command and Its Options
The FORMAT command rearranges the random magnetic impulses on the disk—or the data that are already recorded—into a series of tracks and sectors.

These are examples of opposite extremes. The first example does not explain enough, and the second explains too much. The reader ought to become familiar with the idea of tracks at least, but the overly technical discourse into "random magnetic impulses" smells suspiciously of an author showing off how bright and knowledgeable he is, providing superfluous and largely useless information. The typical owner of a computer can gain nothing but confusion from this unnecessary and undesired information. That information belongs in a physics textbook, which the occasional interested party will hunt up soon enough; it is grossly misplaced here. (If there were to be a choice between the two, I would opt for the first one, since it is all most readers truly need to know.)

There are no rules for this—human judgment is needed to judge which is the necessary depth of detail and which are the appropriate details. In this case, both manuals are designed to aid the PC owner, who is not a computer professional, but merely an average consumer-owner, in mastering his system. In the case cited here the first example is from the manual supplied with the computer, and the second from a good-quality commercial manual published to help the reader for whom the original manual is not quite good enough.

This is an exceptional case, where the manufacturer's manual is superior. Actually, the commercial manual is quite a good one, far better generally than the manufacturer's manual, in most respects. The author was simply carried away a bit in introducing the FORMAT command. The opposite effect is the case when each explains the MORE command. The original manual defines it by the simple statement "The MORE command sends output to the monitor screen one screen at a time," a statement almost certified to be cryptic to any but the most experienced user. The commercial manual uses several sentences of explanation and an example to make clear what MORE does, in exact enough terms to enable the reader to begin using the command immediately. The first statement would give no hint as to how to actually use the command. The reader who is not truly expert in computer usage would have no way of knowing exactly how the command must be formatted. However, the commercial manual not only presents the specific format required—MORE [filename.ext]—but explains what the result will be, illustrates it, and explains how to execute the necessary follow-up commands so that nothing is left to the reader's imagination.

Assembly Instructions

Assembly instructions are the most basic and most common needs in user manuals, whether written for the lay consumer or for the trained specialist.

THE FIRST STEP: KNOWING THE READER

You must have a good understanding of the reader's needs before you can plan a manual of any kind, much less write it. That begins with knowing who the reader is. In terms of assembly instructions, that reader will necessarily always be in one of two basic classes, the technical-professional specialist or the lay consumer. Even that is only the beginning of getting a profile on the reader: You will also need to have a reasonably accurate indication of the reader's technical knowledge, literacy, and relevant experience, if you are to establish an effective communication. (Effective communication means more than language and explanations the reader can understand; it means supplying all the information the reader needs to accomplish the purpose for which the manual is intended.) You can start with division into one of those two classes, lay consumer and relevant specialist of some sort. Even with that rough classification the two classes are poles apart in a great many ways when it comes to writing user instructions for them, and that distinction or accurate identification of the user group to which the reader belongs is a first and important definition for planning.

PRELIMINARY PLANNING

Certain basics of preliminary planning are common to all classes and types of manual. The two critical identifications to be made immediately are the purpose of the manual and the reader. This appears obvious, as in the case of preparing an assembly sheet for a bar stool. The reader is "obviously" an average male consumer who at least knows a screwdriver from a hammer and a pair of pliers from a monkey wrench, and the purpose of the manual is to explain the assembly of the bar stool.

In this case, the assembly is so simple that the bulk of the instruction is a simple sketch of the underside of the seat, to which the metal swivel plate is to be attached by the four bolts included, with only a few lines of text. Unfortunately, however, the writer of the instructions never validated the prescribed procedure by actually assembling one of the stools. Therefore, the writer never learned that the holes in the swivel plate did not align perfectly with the threaded receptacles into which the bolts were to be screwed, and so failed to explain the proper procedure—to only *start* each bolt and not attempt to tighten them until all four were started. (The writer also failed to grasp the significance of the fact that the mounting holes in the swivel plate were slotted to allow some tolerance for a slight imprecision in alignment.)

The assumption was incorrect; the assembly was relatively simple, but not quite as uncomplicated as the writer assumed. Moreover, the assumption that the reader would be a man is unjustified—in today's society there are many single householders who are women. In fact, there are many women who are far more capable of using hand tools effectively and carrying out assembly procedures than their husbands are. It is a false assumption that women do not do such work in their own households.

The bar stool example represents a relatively minor case. The problem is greatly magnified when the manual must describe procedures for assembling a major piece of equipment or a complete system that may require more than one assembler—perhaps an entire crew—and weeks, even months, of work to complete the assembly. Here, the identification of the user—the reader, who is to do the assembly—is far more critical. What does the reader already know—in technical knowledge, that is—and what technical information does he or she need to do the assembly? This question frequently leads to vigorously expressed differences of opinion among the writing and planning staffs.

The answer is never easy. It can even lead to another question: Should the technical information—which is deemed necessary, but only indirectly related to the assembly operations—be supplied along with the assembly instructions? Or should the reader be advised to read the functional description and theory information in a separate chapter or a separate manual? Typically, operators, assemblers, and installers of equipment systems are not technical experts to the same degree that is required of maintenance specialists, but there are exceptions to this. And, there is at least one other important consideration that may be linked to the question of what an assembler needs in the way of technical knowledge: is the assembler likely to be the same individual who will be the operator and/or maintainer of the system?

COMMON AND UNCOMMON FACTORS

If there is any most common factor in user instructions, it is the need for assembly guidance. Even at the extremes of the two kinds of cases considered here the two have a few common needs, including the following:

- Each needs a graphic description—drawing(s) or photograph(s)—of what the final assembly should be and how it should appear.
- Each needs a listing of parts and materials to enable the user to check and verify that all are present.
- Both need explanations or listings of tools, materials, and/or other necessities not included in the package as delivered.
- Both need procedural guidance for the assembly, including procedures for subassemblies when appropriate.

After that, the road parts; there are substantial differences in the manuals. The following is a brief summary of major differences, beginning with the typical needs and factors in instructions for assembling a typical consumer item. (The exception is the item for which there are many aficionados or hobbyists who are as expert as the professionals, i.e., radio "ham" operators and computer "hackers.")

- The item itself will be a relatively simple one.
- The assembly will require only ordinary hand tools, such as might be found in most households—pliers, screwdriver, hammer, and similar tools.
- The specific procedures can be illustrated in words and in simple line drawings.
- The assembly will require absolutely no special technical knowledge of any kind.
- There is no special hazard, other than the possibility of a minor cut or abrasion, likely to be incurred in the assembly.

On the other hand, writing assembly instructions for technical specialists or the expert hobbyists referred to earlier is another matter. The conditions are likely to include at least some of the following:

- The item will be fairly complex, perhaps even highly technical in nature.
- Special tools will be required.
- The assembly may require prior site preparation, such as a poured base, provision of special utilities, special housing, or other construction.
- Despite detailed instructions, success in assembly will depend in large part on the special training and skills of the assembler(s).
- The assembly is likely to require periodic testing during assembly and final testing at conclusion to verify success.

SUGGESTED OUTLINE

The following is a suggested outline for an assembly manual. This is a generalized approach, based on the assumption of a full-scale, independent assembly manual. The sequence of items listed may easily be varied, and the outline may be modified as necessary and adapted to individual cases, using the guidance of Table 5–1 and your own judgment. The outline and table may also be used as a checklist to help in developing your own, independent outlines and plans.

TABLE 5–1. Items That Should Be Included in Assembly Instructions

Item	Expert User	Inexpert User
Specifications for site preparation*	X	X
Complete list of parts included	X	X
Descriptions/drawings of parts	X	X
List of hardware (e.g., nuts and bolts) included	X	X
Description/drawings of hardware		X
List of hardware needed, but not included	X	X
List of common hand tools needed		X
Descriptions/drawings of common hand tools needed		X
List/descriptions of special tools needed†	X	X
Line drawing, with callouts/notes, of assembled unit	X	X
Exploded views/illustrated parts breakdown drawings	X	X
Text listings of procedural steps and sequence	X	X
Text references to relevant drawings	X	X
Notes on safety relevant to assembly procedures	X	X
Special notes, cautions, do's and don'ts lists	X	X

*Site preparation is usually required only for major system installations.
†It is not likely that items intended for lay users will often require special tools for their assembly.

It is beneficial to both the user and the writer to utilize the idea of subassemblies wherever possible, even in the case of relatively simple and uncomplicated end-items because it breaks the entire procedure down into simpler steps and a simpler progression. If, for example, hinges are to be fastened to a lid or door, and the door then fastened to a cabinet, it is helpful to make the door and first steps of fastening the hinges to it a subassembly. Similarly, if site preparation is involved, it should be treated as a separate subject and separate set of specifications.

The outline and table are followed by discussions of the principal areas identified in and by the outline and table.

I. Introduction.
    A. Identification of item.
        1. Description.
            a. Of equipment/system.
            b. Of site requirements.
        2. Reference to illustration(s).
        3. Characteristics relevant to identification.
        4. Reference to related information found elsewhere.
    B. General observations regarding assembly.
        1. Assemblies, if subassemblies required.
        2. Special notes regarding procedures and/or sequence.
        3. Notes regarding site preparation.
        4. Special safety precautions, if any.
II. Before beginning assembly.
    A. Site preparation.
        1. Specifications.
        2. Illustrations.
        3. Procedures.

    B. Parts and/or components.
        1. Standard parts/components.
        2. Special/custom parts/components.
    C. Tools required.
        1. Common tools.
        2. Special tools.
    D. Procedures.
        1. Sequence of assembly.
        2. Special notes, cautions, warnings.
        3. Final checks.

INTRODUCTION AND IDENTIFICATION

Introductions may vary from simply naming and illustrating the item to detailed descriptions and specifications, according to the nature, size, and cost of the item. A Sears manual on a pushbutton memory telephone begins with a page of cautions against attempting to service the instrument's internal parts. It also includes a warning of possible dangerous voltage, and it stresses paying attention to the important operating instructions that follow. Then, under the title *Introduction*, a brief paragraph assures the reader of the high quality of the instrument and is followed by a list of 17 items explaining the various functions and features of the instrument. The description following is a series of three line drawings of the telephone, top and bottom views, identifying all the controls, switches, and connectors.

Pros and Cons of Line Drawings versus Photographs

You have a choice of two basic options in illustrations: photographs and line drawings. Photographs are often less expensive to create, especially when the item is a fairly complex one. In some cases they make it easier for the reader to recognize the item. However, line drawings are a better choice because they are less costly to print than photographs but, more important, they usually provide clearer instruction for the reader than photographs. Photographs tend to have distracting and irrelevant elements, and they do not always reproduce well. The line drawing, on the other hand, permits you to concentrate on and show only the significant elements without those distractions.

Resources for Drawings

Creating a line drawing may be slightly less expensive than photographing objects in some cases. Some photographs, such as those for various stages of assembly, may require extensive and fairly elaborate staging and even human models, whereas most line drawings—even an illustrated parts breakdown or exploded view—are simpler to create and to understand. It does not necessarily require costly professional illustrators to create good line drawings; there are inexpensive alternatives to be found in any well-stocked art-supplies emporium (including many do-it-yourself materials), and in many cases these are entirely appropriate to and suitable for the needs of assembly instructions. (Between the many templates and ready-made art, such as clip-art books, clip-art computer programs, and decalcomania or transfer art—it is often possible for anyone to create line drawings of professional or near-professional quality.) There is also the availability of computer clip art, illustrations that you can generate via your own personal computer, with suitable desktop-publishing software. Figure 5–1 is an excellent example of a simple, clear line drawing that is entirely suitable for assembly instructions. The entire item, with all its parts, is shown in a single drawing that also identifies each part and the relationships of all to each other. The text (Figure 5–2) suggests the recommended order of assembly and amplifies the implied instructions of the drawing, but it is possible to assemble the item from the drawing alone if the assembler has some familiarity with such work and relevant hand tools. No doubt the creator of these assembly instructions intended the drawing to be the primary means of instruction, as it should be.

That illustrates another point about using line drawings, especially exploded views such as that of Figure 5–1: The illustration is equally useful for the expert and the beginner. The text is available to aid the reader who needs that aid, but the expert can work from the drawing alone and need not be slowed down by reading text.

Another excellent example of instructions conveyed largely by line drawings is shown in Figure 5–3. The instructions cover the assembly and installation of an electric floor fan. I found this to be one assembly—almost a rarity—that went without a hitch. In fact, although an assembly sequence is recommended by the text, almost any sequence can be used, simply following the simple, but completely clear, line drawings showing the assembly in an illustrated parts breakdown.

INSTRUCTIONS FOR MORE COMPLEX EQUIPMENT

The problem is considerably more complex when addressing the assembly of a larger and more complex item, such as the Black & Decker belt and disc sander. For this the manufacturer's assembly instructions, pages 5 through 8 of a 12-page Instruction Manual, offer more than a dozen line drawings and a rather stern admonition to follow the sequence and directions given. In fact, the procedure is broken down into several elements and subassemblies, including assembly of the stand, installation of the motor, installation of the switch box, and installation of the sander assembly.

Combinations of Text and Drawings

In this case, many of the textual instructions are included as part of the drawings. Figure 5–4 illustrates part of this manual, showing a mix of drawing techniques in providing instructions for assembling the

FIGURE 5–1 Assembly Instructions for Toy Truck (sheet 1)

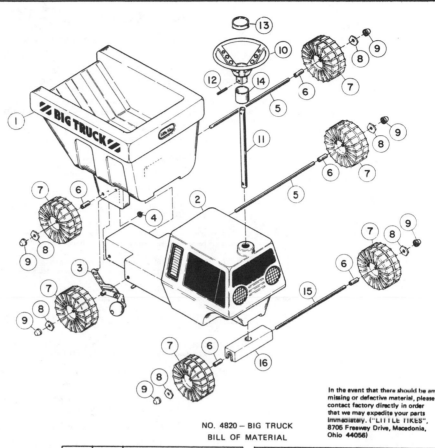

NO. 4820 – BIG TRUCK
BILL OF MATERIAL

In the event that there should be any missing or defective material, please contact factory directly in order that we may expedite your parts immediately. ("LITTLE TIKES", 8705 Freeway Drive, Macedonia, Ohio 44056)

ITEM	QTY,	DESCRIPTION
1	1	Dumper Section
2	1	Big Truck Body
3	1	Dumper Control
4	1	Push On Fastener
5	2	Long (Center & Rear Axle) 12"
6	5	Spacer
7	6	Wheel
8	6	Hex Washer
9	6	Red Push Nut ¼"

ITEM	QTY.	DESCRIPTION
10	1	Steering Wheel
11	1	Steering Shaft
12	1	Roll Pin
13	1	White Horn Button
14	1	Black Spacer
15	1	Short (Front) Axle 11 3/16"
16	1	Axle Housing
17	2	Big Truck Decals
18	1	Window Decals Sheet

APPLICATION OF LETTERS

Clean surface of unit thoroughly. Peel & separate smooth paper backing from textured paper "carrier sheet". Place letters (adhesive side) to body of unit in location as shown on carton. Apply pressure with hand or hard object in pressing letters firmly against unit. Slowly peel at sharp angle textured "carrier sheet" surface away from unit and letters will remain in place.

If when peeling, a letter remains with "paper carrier", and does not sitck to unit, once again press letter against unit and apply more pressure for proper adherence.

Repeat process with second decal to complete other side of unit.

stand. The manual's Figure 1 simply identifies components of the stand, with separate text explaining the procedures. The next figure of the manual, however, illustrates the assembly procedure and includes instructions in the drawing.

Since the end-item is a fairly complex assembly, an orientation drawing of the entire assembly is virtually a necessity, so that the user may visualize the locations of the various subassemblies with respect to each other and the end-item. Such a drawing is furnished in the manual

FIGURE 5–2 Assembly Instructions for Toy Truck (sheet 2)

NO. 4820 – BIG TRUCK

ASSEMBLY INSTRUCTIONS

NO. 4820 – BIG TRUCK

TOOLS NEEDED: Screw Driver, Hammer or Rubber Mallet

1.   Insert stem on end of Dumper Control (3) into forward hole located on right tab under Dumper Section (11). Secure control to dumper with Push On Fastener (4).

2.   Locate Dumper Section (1) on rear of Big Truck Body (2) and align pre-drilled holes on bottom tabs of dumper with those, furthest to the rear, on body.

3.   Insert one Long Axle (5) into aligned holes, locking together both dumper and body sections.

4.   Slide Spacer (6) on each end of axle.

5.   Attach Wheel (7) to each end of axle, followed by Hex Washer (8). Secure each end with a Red Push Nut (9).

6.   Align pivot hole on Dumper Control (3) with right pre-drilled hole remaining at rear of body. Insert long axle through holes holding control in place.

7.   Slide spacer (6) on other end of axle protruding out left side of body. Attach wheel to each end of axle, followed by hex washer and secure each end with red push nut.

8.   Attach Steering Wheel (10) to Steering Shaft (11) by inserting end of shaft with smaller hole into bottom of steering wheel hub.

9.   Align holes of hub with those in shaft. Secure together by inserting roll pin (12) into hex recess on side of wheel hub, through aligned holes.

10. Snap White Horn Button (13) into recessed hole at top of steering whee. Be sure tabs of button engage into slots at bottom of recess.

11. Insert steering shaft assembly into hole at top of Big Truck cab and bring out through hole at bottom.

12. Insert end of steering shaft into hole at top of Axle Housing (16) and align holes of shaft with axle slot along bottom of housing.

13. Insert Short Axle (15) along housings slot and through holes in steering shaft.

14. Slide spacer on each end of axle. Attach wheel to each end of axle followed by hex washer and secure each end with red push nut.

15. Carefully apply decals on locations shown in illustration.

(shown here as Figure 5–5), along with a description of parts. (Nine parts are listed in the table that accompanies the figure, and all are also identified by callouts in the drawing, along with six other parts called out in the drawing but not listed in the table.)

As in the case of many other user instructions, safety, installation, and operating instructions are occasionally given in the assembly section, particularly when that helps the user to understand the significance of the part or subassembly.

FIGURE 5–3 Instructions for Assembling Electric Fan

ASSEMBLING INSTRUCTIONS

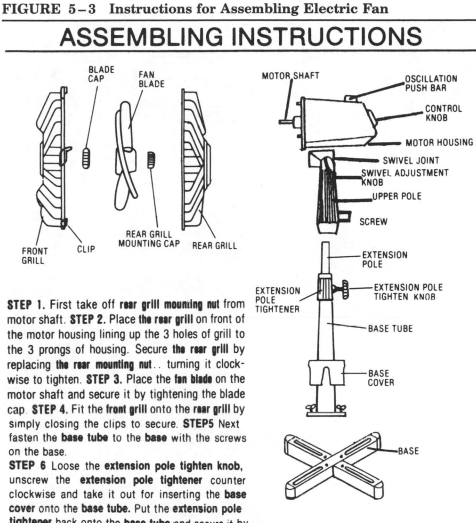

STEP 1. First take off **rear grill mounting nut** from motor shaft. **STEP 2.** Place **the rear grill** on front of the motor housing lining up the 3 holes of grill to the 3 prongs of housing. Secure **the rear grill** by replacing **the rear mounting nut**.. turning it clockwise to tighten. **STEP 3.** Place the **fan blade** on the motor shaft and secure it by tightening the blade cap. **STEP 4.** Fit the **front grill** onto the **rear grill** by simply closing the clips to secure. **STEP5** Next fasten the **base tube** to the **base** with the screws on the base.

STEP 6 Loose the **extension pole tighten knob,** unscrew the **extension pole tightener** counter clockwise and take it out for inserting the **base cover** onto the **base tube.** Put the **extension pole tightener** back onto the **base tube** and secure it by turning clockwise. Pull up the **extension pole** to desired height and fasten the **extension tighten knob.** **STEP 7** Insert **upper pole** to top of **extension pole.** Tighten **screw** through holes.

Reasonable Premises

Note here that no mention is made of identifying the common hand tools and assembly hardware required for assembly of the sander. That is because a woodworking power tool such as this is not exactly a typical consumer item. The individual who buys this kind of item is an experienced and knowledgeable user of such tools, whether a professional or hobbyist. This user needs no introduction to common hand tools and ordinary hardware items.

For this reason, hand tools are mentioned only in passing here; it is assumed—reasonably so—that the user will know what tools to use when the instructions refer to "two $7/32$" wrenches, tape measure, and an adjustable wrench, and what fastening hardware is referred to when

FIGURE 5-4   A Portion of Assembly Instructions for a Sander

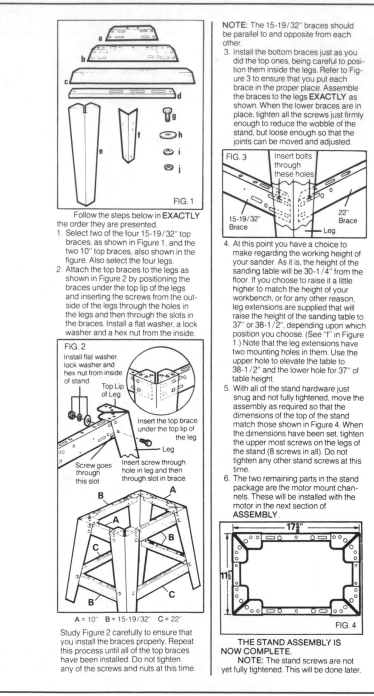

Follow the steps below in **EXACTLY** the order they are presented.

1. Select two of the four 15-19/32" top braces, as shown in Figure 1, and the two 10" top braces, also shown in the figure. Also select the four legs.

2. Attach the top braces to the legs as shown in Figure 2 by positioning the braces under the top lip of the legs and inserting the screws from the outside of the legs through the holes in the legs and then through the slots in the braces. Install a flat washer, a lock washer and a hex nut from the inside.

Study Figure 2 carefully to ensure that you install the braces properly. Repeat this process until all of the top braces have been installed. Do not tighten any of the screws and nuts at this time.

NOTE: The 15-19/32" braces should be parallel to and opposite from each other.

3. Install the bottom braces just as you did the top ones, being careful to position them inside the legs. Refer to Figure 3 to ensure that you put each brace in the proper place. Assemble the braces to the legs **EXACTLY** as shown. When the lower braces are in place, tighten all the screws just firmly enough to reduce the wobble of the stand, but loose enough so that the joints can be moved and adjusted.

4. At this point you have a choice to make regarding the working height of your sander. As it is, the height of the sanding table will be 30-1/4" from the floor. If you choose to raise it a little higher to match the height of your workbench, or for any other reason, leg extensions are supplied that will raise the height of the sanding table to 37" or 38-1/2", depending upon which position you choose. (See "f" in Figure 1.) Note that the leg extensions have two mounting holes in them. Use the upper hole to elevate the table to 38-1/2" and the lower hole for 37" of table height.

5. With all of the stand hardware just snug and not fully tightened, move the assembly as required so that the dimensions of the top of the stand match those shown in Figure 4. When the dimensions have been set, tighten the upper most screws on the legs of the stand (8 screws in all). Do not tighten any other stand screws at this time.

6. The two remaining parts in the stand package are the motor mount channels. These will be installed with the motor in the next section of **ASSEMBLY**.

THE STAND ASSEMBLY IS NOW COMPLETE.
   NOTE: The stand screws are not yet fully tightened. This will be done later.

Courtesy Black & Decker, Inc.

FIGURE 5–5 Completely Assembled Power Sander

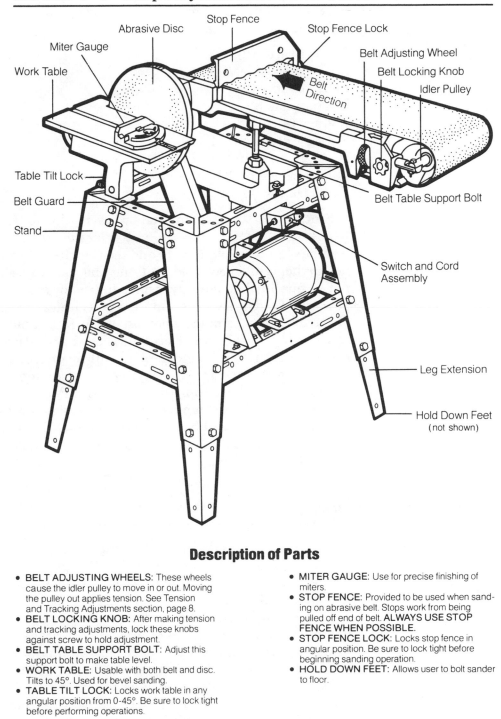

Stop Fence
Abrasive Disc
Stop Fence Lock
Miter Gauge
Belt Adjusting Wheel
Work Table
Belt Locking Knob
Idler Pulley
Belt Direction
Table Tilt Lock
Belt Guard
Belt Table Support Bolt
Stand
Switch and Cord Assembly
Leg Extension
Hold Down Feet (not shown)

Description of Parts

- **BELT ADJUSTING WHEELS:** These wheels cause the idler pulley to move in or out. Moving the pulley out applies tension. See Tension and Tracking Adjustments section, page 8.
- **BELT LOCKING KNOB:** After making tension and tracking adjustments, lock these knobs against screw to hold adjustment.
- **BELT TABLE SUPPORT BOLT:** Adjust this support bolt to make table level.
- **WORK TABLE:** Usable with both belt and disc. Tilts to 45°. Used for bevel sanding.
- **TABLE TILT LOCK:** Locks work table in any angular position from 0-45°. Be sure to lock tight before performing operations.

- **MITER GAUGE:** Use for precise finishing of miters.
- **STOP FENCE:** Provided to be used when sanding on abrasive belt. Stops work from being pulled off end of belt. **ALWAYS USE STOP FENCE WHEN POSSIBLE.**
- **STOP FENCE LOCK:** Locks stop fence in angular position. Be sure to lock tight before beginning sanding operation.
- **HOLD DOWN FEET:** Allows user to bolt sander to floor.

Courtesy Black & Decker, Inc.

instructed to "Install a flat washer, a lock washer, and a hex nut from the inside." On the other hand, parts are listed. The parts for the stand, for example, are listed as follows:

a. 10" Braces (2).
b. 15–$^{19}/_{32}$" Braces (4).
c. 22" Braces (2).
d. Channels (2).
e. Legs (4).
f. Leg Extensions (4).
g. ¼" 20 x ½" Hex Head Screws (32).
h. Flat Washers (32).
i. ¼" Hex Nuts (32).

Since no further explanation or description of these parts is provided it is rather obvious that the writer assumed that the user—reader— would be quite mechanically and technically literate and would require no further guidance in identifying the parts needed. (Those who are not so qualified do not buy, aspire to use, or attempt to assemble large power tools.) The same assumption of technical and mechanical literacy of the user may be made when an organization buys equipment for use in their business or other organizational activities. It is reasonable to assume that if your customers are all business organizations of some sort—an airport authority buying an instrument landing system, a corporation buying a computer, or a military organization buying a new radar system, for example—whoever is assigned to the assembly (the true user, that is) will be someone well qualified in all respects and not a layperson. This assumption is a governing principle for the design of your user instructions.

ASSEMBLY SEQUENCE

A first item to consider in prescribing the specific steps and operations in the assembly is the sequence of the steps. In many cases, especially where the item to be assembled is a rather simple one, there is no special significance to the sequence in which the item is assembled; the sequence can be entirely arbitrary. Frequently, in assembling simple items, the proper sequence of assembly is readily apparent on casual inspection. In the case of the Black & Decker power sander, for example, it is rather obvious that you cannot mount the motor or other components on the stand before you have assembled the stand. However, there are many cases where the proper sequence is not self-evident but, if the proper sequence is not followed, it becomes a truth that "you can't get there from here." One missed, neglected, or misunderstood step in an assembly sequence may require the user to disassemble or undo everything already accomplished and go back to the first step again. And human nature being what it is, there is a great deal of truth in the jest, "When all else fails, read the instructions." Many of us, if not most of us, tend to hurry on, relying on the drawings and, perhaps to an even larger extent on our observation and perception of what is a logical sequence, hasten through the assembly with hardly more than a glance at the written instructions. (We turn to the instructions, then, only when we have finally perceived that we are in difficulties and are not going to get there from here!) If some given sequence is essential to a successful assembly, a prominent notice to that effect is in order. That notice ought to be prominently displayed so that the user is all but certain to see it as a first thing when examining the assembly instructions. Something like Figure 5–6 is suggested, and it ought to be as near the beginning of the assembly instructions as possible. It might even be suitable on the title page of the assembly instructions. It is then important to make the assembly sequence absolutely clear in both text and illustrations. (You must be at pains to help the user comply with the notice.)

One Assembly or Several?

Where the end-item is complex or relatively complex and the assembly procedure therefore somewhat complicated, the procedure often consists of more than one stage of assembly. That is, it often requires putting together two or more subassemblies and then marrying all into a final assembly. In such case, this assembly philosophy of successive sub-assemblies and a final assembly should be made clear to the user at once. The user can comprehend and follow the procedural instructions more easily when he or she understands the basic assembly strategy.

VALIDATION OF PROCEDURES

Unfortunately, the prescribed procedures for assembly are not always validated. Instead, writers prescribe what they believe to be a sensible and logical assembly procedure, but never validate the procedure by actual tryout. With the possible exception of the simplest end-items and simplest assembly operations, the procedures should always be written as a rough draft and then validated. Validation is achieved by actually using the instructions to perform an assembly of the end-item to see whether they do work satisfactorily. It is surprising how often you can overlook some small thing that then invalidates your prescribed procedure.

FIGURE 5–6 Suggested Notice

NOTICE
IT IS ABSOLUTELY NECESSARY TO FOLLOW THE ASSEMBLY SEQUENCE PRESCRIBED IN THESE IN-STRUCTIONS. FAILURE TO DO SO WILL RESULT IN DIFFICULTY IN COMPLETING THE ASSEMBLY SUC-CESSFULLY.

Chapter 6

Installation Instructions

Even defining installation, *let alone explaining it, is not a simple matter, but it is necessary to do both.*

INSTALLATION AS AN ARBITRARY CLASSIFICATION

Installation and assembly are such closely related functions that in some cases one cannot be discussed effectively without discussing the other. In fact, both must be carried out together in many cases. They are thus often inseparable, virtually identical subjects, as noted earlier. As a further complication, installation and assembly may sometimes involve procedures that in another case would be covered under operating instructions. That leads to a problem of sorts in discussing the three types of manuals, especially those for assembly and installation: They overlap to the extent that certain subjects, such as site preparation, are common to both and might be covered in either manual, according to the individual circumstances and characteristics of the item. On the other hand, your own needs or choice may be for only one of these manuals or sets of instructions. Therefore, the redundancies here are deliberate, to make each discussion for a type of manual complete in itself.

WHAT IS INSTALLATION?

The meaning of installation varies widely with different applications. In many cases where installation instructions are provided (as defined here) that word is not used to describe or categorize the instructions referred to. It is therefore necessary to first establish what the word means in its usage here. And it is necessary to acknowledge, also, that not every item sold truly requires installation instructions by any reasonable definition of the word, even if the item does require some other kind of user instructions. The installation of a TV stand, shaving mirror, or minor stand-alone appliance is readily apparent to any adult. On the other hand, an electric broom sold by Sears requires only the minor final assembly or installation of fastening the handle and cord hook (see Figure 6–1). But installing major systems, such as a heating plant or ventilation system, involves extensive installation, with site preparation and concurrent assembly. The latter system is made up of many components, rather than a single unit. Those represent physical installation in the latter case. There is also the question of installing intangibles, such as software systems or inventory-control programs.

A SUGGESTED OUTLINE

As in the case of assembly instructions, the suggested outline offered here for installation instructions is based on the presumption of a full-scale manual that covers all possible needs. And, as in the case of assembly, few actual cases would require such extensive coverage. So the outline offered here is intended as a basic model to be modified and adapted by whatever changes are necessary to fit any given set of circumstances. This outline may also be used as a checklist if you prefer to develop a completely new outline of your own. Where the same topic is covered here that is covered in another outline you must use your own judgment as to which of your manuals it belongs in. It is included here simply to ensure that you do not have to search elsewhere for the information.

The discussions that follow throughout the remainder of this chapter are based on the outline and its flow of information.

    I.   Preliminary orientation.
        A.   Description of item.
            1. Purpose.
            2. Physical size, shape, dimensions.
            3. Functional—operating principle(s).
        B.   Notes.
            1. Unusual features.
            2. Precautions.
   II.   Site preparation.
        A.   Description of work space required.
        B.   Excavation(s) required.
        C.   Base or foundation required.
        D.   Other special requirements.
  III.   Tools and materials.
        A.   Parts and components required.
            1. Supplied elements.
            2. Assembly hardware and fasteners.
            3. Other materials than those supplied.
        B.   Tools and special equipment needed.
            1. Ordinary hand tools.
            2. Special hand tools.

FIGURE 6–1 Installation Instructions for an Electric Broom

ASSEMBLY INSTRUCTIONS

— Unpack the vacuum cleaner from the carton. Indertify the parts shown below. (fig. A) Remove and dispose of the cardboard packing.

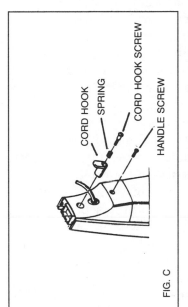

HANDLE ASSEMBLY

HOUSING

AIR INLET

FLOOR TCOL

FIG. A

— There are 6 screws in the fastener package. The three different type screws and their uses are described below. (fig. B)

CORD HOOK SCREW (1 REQ.)

HANDLE SCREW (1 REQ.)

AIR INLET SCREW (4 REQ.)

FIG. B

1. Insert handle into rectangular opening in the top of the housing. Make sure the grip area of the handle is facing the back of the vacuum cleaner as shown on cover photo. Push the handle into this hole until the screw holes in the handle are visible through the holes in the housing. Insert the handle screw (fig. B) into the lowest hole and tighten firmly.

2. Slide, first, the spring then the cord hook onto the cord hook screw. Insert this assembly into the upper hole in the housing and tighten firmly (fig. C).

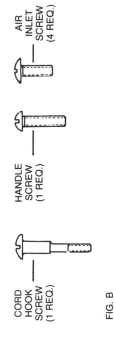

CORD HOOK

SPRING

CORD HOOK SCREW

HANDLE SCREW

FIG. C

3. To assemble the air inlet, you must first READ then REMOVE the red label on the bottom of the housing. This label is in place to warn you that the impeller is located just inside this opening in the housing. **The air inlet should NEVER be put on or taken off of the vacuum cleaner while it is plugged in.** The impeller rotates very rapidly and can cause injury to the operator if the vacuum cleaner is accidently turned on without the air inlet in place.

Fasten the air inlet to the bottom of the main body with the 4 air inlet screws (fig. B). Make sure that all screws are tightened secured.

4. The floor tool slides onto the air inlet so that the corners on the air inlet line up with the corners on the floor tool. Tap firmly on the bottom of the floor tool with your hand to make sure the floor tool is firmly in place on the air inlet.

Part # 62935A

        3. Power tools.

        4. Special equipment.

           a. Mechanical.

           b. Electrical.

           c. Electronic.

    C. Special jigs and fixtures.

    D. Other/miscellaneous.

  IV. Installation procedures.

    A. Preliminary explanations.

        1. Preinstallation steps (e.g., subassemblies, stripping wires).

        2. Notes on installation sequence(s).

        3. Cautions and warnings.

    B. Procedural steps.

        1. Physical activities.

        2. Notes on verifying correctness before proceeding.

   V. Adjustments and tuning.

    A. Explanations of adjustments and tuning.

        1. General philosophy of procedures.

        2. When, where, what assemblies/subassemblies to be adjusted.

        3. Procedures (talk-through).

  VI. Checks and verification.

    A. Review and checklist to verify all adjustments.

    B. Preview of next step.

 VII. Testing.

    A. Explanation/rationales for tests.

        1. For tests at subassembly or intermediate levels.

        2. For tests at system levels.

    B. Test procedures.

        1. For tests at subassembly or intermediate levels.

        2. For tests at system levels.

VIII. Certification.

    A. Explanation of requirements for certification.

    B. Explanation of certification procedures.

  IX. Initial operation.

    A. Explanation/discussion of initial operation.

    B. Initial-operation procedures.

   X. Training customer personnel.

    A. Explanation of the training philosophy.

        1. Subjects to be taught.

           a. Functional theory.

           b. Design considerations.

           c. Operating principles and procedures.

           d. Maintenance principles.

           e. Maintenance procedures.

           f. Management of system.

    B. Description of training materials.

        1. Documentation.

           a. General.

           b. Special.

PRELIMINARY ORIENTATION

Whether the reader requires an orientation section depends on several factors: If the installation instructions are a section or subsection within a more general document, it may be assumed that the reader was oriented by an earlier, introductory section of the document. Otherwise, if the installation instructions are a separate manual, it must be assumed that the reader will not have read or perhaps even had access to general introductory and descriptive material. So the reader will need such an orientation as a first or preparatory step and an integral part of the installation instructions. On the other hand, many installations are simple and do not truly require a general orientation except, perhaps, a photograph or drawing of the assembled end-item or a brief word description of what the end-item (or system) will be. That may also depend on whether the installation instructions are intended for reading and use by a layperson or by a technical specialist of some sort. Obviously, the layperson will require far more extensive orientation than someone who is especially qualified as a technical specialist. The term *technical specialist,* as contrasted with and distinguished from the term *layperson,* requires some explanation: The term refers to any and all who have relevant specialized knowledge, training, and/or experience. It includes both those who are literally technical specialists— engineers, scientists, programmers, and technicians—and executives in purchasing, financial management, production control, quality assurance, inventory systems, and other relevant specialties that are not, strictly speaking, technical specialties.

SITE PREPARATION

Some installations require special preparation of sites, such as the installation or availability of certain utilities (power, light, sewers, drains, etc), the pouring of foundations upon which to mount heavy equipment, special requirements concerning enclosures, or other items. Of course it may also be as simple as advising the user that the item must be installed for use adjacent to an ordinary electrical outlet or kitchen sink. *Site preparation* is therefore a rather broad term, interpreted to suit the circumstances. Where site preparation is a major task it will usually be covered by separate instructions and specifications.

ASSEMBLING OF EQUIPMENT/COMPONENTS/TOOLS

Assembling is not the same term as *assembly*. Assembling equipment, components, and tools is a preliminary step to installation. It calls for laying out all those items, ready to use in the installation processes. However, it may very well include carrying out some assembly procedures that are concurrent with and hardly distinguishable from installation procedures. The objective is, primarily, to let the user know in advance what items of equipment, components, parts, and tools are necessary to perform and complete the installation successfully. This is so that the user may prepare and have everything ready before beginning installation. Having everything ready and at hand in advance helps greatly in achieving an efficient installation. Moreover, in some cases it may be necessary for the user to procure tools or equipment that the user does not have readily available. The advance notice that such items are needed is an important one.

INSTALLATION PROCEDURES

Obviously the specific procedures must be explained, whether by a line drawing with suitable notations or via a lengthy and thick manual. Procedures must be given in some order that relates to the order in which the end-item is to be installed. The proper sequence of installation procedures must be emphasized as well. (Here, as in the case of assembly, some of the steps presented as installation may actually be assembly procedures.) The procedures should include direction as to which tools to use and include safety reminders, as appropriate.

ADJUSTMENTS AND TUNING

Many items require various adjustments and tuning—even fine-tuning—to achieve a satisfactory installation. These can be literal adjustments and tuning, as in the case of complex electronic systems, and may by themselves constitute extensive and bulky elements within the instructions. In some cases, these may even be the main element of the instructions, although in other cases they are relatively minor, but yet important adjustments. The very terms *adjustment* and *tuning* are philosophical terms and do not necessarily refer to physical adjustments. A financial-management or inventory-control system, for example, would normally have to be adjusted and fine-tuned—adapted—to the individual circumstances of the organization.

TESTING

Testing can be a critical part of an installation. Its purpose is to verify adjustments and operation overall. Again, as in the case of adjustments and tuning, it may very well constitute the bulk of the installation instructions. In many cases the contract will require testing and will specify it in great and exacting detail. And again it may mean making certain technical measurements. But it may also mean running trial balances and simulating true operational situations to judge (as distinct from measuring) the result as a test of the validity of the system.

CERTIFICATION

Certification and/or validation are logical steps following the completion of testing and are, in fact, often the very reason for the testing. They are essentially the same except that validation may be a somewhat informal assurance that all performs as promised. But certification normally is a formal procedure that produces a written affidavit—a certificate—attesting to satisfactory and/or acceptable performance. *Validation,* however, is a term more commonly applied to trying out procedures to verify their validity, whereas *certification* is more suggestive of validating an entire system and bearing sworn witness to that fact.

INITIAL OPERATION

In many cases, in the installation of a system, the seller contracts to operate the system initially for the buyer. Ultimately, the seller will turn the system over to the buyer after the seller has installed, adjusted, debugged, trained the buyer's staff, and validated or certified the system. This is all accomplished during the period when the seller operates the installed system.

TRAINING CUSTOMER PERSONNEL

The obligation to train the customer's staff to operate and/or maintain the installed system is not an uncommon one, even in military contracts. It is a great aid to the buyer, greatly simplifying the problems of owning and operating the system. The seller must usually develop a complete training program for the buyer's personnel, and that may include training in any or all relevant functions—operations, maintenance, and other—and conduct the training. The training is usually based on the user documentation—the various manuals—and may require that special training manuals be developed also, if the training is to be repeated enough times to justify the additional cost.

TURNOVER

The purpose of training buyer personnel is to turn the system and all responsibility for it over to the buyer as the final step of what is commonly referred to as a *turnkey* project or contract. At that point, the seller's responsibility ends, usually, except for any equipment or service warranties that may still exist. While turnover is not usually a subject in and of itself in documenting a system, the prospect of turning over the system should be borne in mind when developing the manuals.

Chapter 7

Operating Instructions

Operating instructions are usually—but not always—the simplest ones to prepare and the briefest portion of the total documentation.

TWO SIGNIFICANT DIFFERENCES

In the case of large systems, the operating instructions are usually the most slender set. In most cases, even in rather large systems, the duties of system operators are far less demanding than the duties of maintenance technicians or even of the installation specialists. Thus operators need not be as expert or as skilled as the others. Not surprisingly, the operating instructions themselves are usually far less voluminous than the instructions for installation and maintenance.

This is equally true for many consumer items, such as television receivers, videocassette recorders, food processors, hair dryers, personal computers, and other items usually sold to buyers who are not technical experts. The user instructions for such items focus on assembly, where appropriate, and on operating procedures. They touch briefly or not at all on maintenance, (other than the minimal maintenance a lay person might perform), reserving true maintenance instructions to separate, technical manuals. In the case of many smaller systems and common consumer goods, there are sometimes no operating instructions at all. This is because many commodities sold in KD (knocked-down) form need not be "operated" at all, but merely assembled and put to use. This chapter is limited to items that have requirements for some significant body of operating principles, procedures, and related data. However, when it is necessary to provide operating instructions, there are several possible requirements:

■ For many relatively simple, small systems only a few specific procedures must be learned. Once learned, they are usually committed to memory with no further reference to the printed instructions necessary. In this case, very little and often no orientation or technical data need be provided, as a rule.

■ In contrast, for large and complex systems, the operator may need to be technically oriented, if not formally trained as a qualified technician. The operating instructions may include formal procedures that must be followed rigidly. In that case, the operating instructions must be in a physical form and format that is suitable for frequent reference by the operator.

■ Where the operator must be formally trained, the operating instructions must usually serve as a training text, as well as a set of reference materials. (In some cases the operators may be trained from the same texts used for training maintenance technicians.)

■ Where there is a formalized set of procedures for operating a system, and especially where the operator is to be trained formally, the operator is likely to have some minimal or operator-level maintenance requirement. This includes routine inspections, checking trouble lights and indicators, and reporting all conditions. In such case, the operating instructions must include relevant maintenance instructions.

Computer software programs, for example, offer good illustrations of two basic sets of circumstances. There are very simple programs that do very simple jobs, such as listing all the files on a disk, along with some useful information about each file. Operating such a program requires only knowledge of a simple command, such as "DIR," to be typed on the keyboard, with an understanding of what the information on the screen means. Obviously, it is easy to memorize the single, simple command. On the other hand, operating a complete word processing program, such as *WordStar*® or Lotus 1-2-3™ requires even experienced experts in the systems to keep the manual at hand to look up some of the commands, which are too numerous for most people to memorize completely. There has been a distinct trend in recent years to include special tutorials—demonstration programs and exercises—to help the reader learn the system quickly.

A SUGGESTED OUTLINE

Although brief compared with some of the other outlines, a great many kinds of operating instructions and procedural guides are suggested in the following outline of suggested content for documentation of operating instructions. As in the cases of earlier outlines offered—in fact, perhaps to an even greater extent—this one is offered as a catch-all model, to be adapted to whatever uses and needs you encounter or to serve as a checklist for writing your own outline.

    I. Introduction.
        A. Philosophical observations.
            1. General nature of item/equipment/system.
            2. Modernity of design.
            3. Other.
        B. General descriptive narrative.
            1. Functional highlights.
               a. Speed.
               b. Convenience.

    2. Controls and indicators.
        a. Switches—pushbutton, toggle, rotary, other.
        b. Indicators—meters, lamps, LEDs, LCDs, other.
    3. Safety features/cautions/notes.
II. Operating procedures.
  A. Normal operations.
    1. Startup sequence.
        a. Controls—locations, positions, sequences.
        b. Indicators—locations, normal indications.
    2. Typical operation after startup.
        a. Controls—locations, positions, uses of.
        b. Indicators—location, signals of normal operation.
    3. Operations highlights.
    4. Safety precautions.
    5. Normal shutdown.
        a. Steps.
        b. Sequence.
        c. Securing after normal shutdown.
  B. Emergency operations.
    1. Limited operation with reduced capacity.
        a. Indications of malfunction.
        b. Operational sequence for operating at reduced capacity.
    2. Operation under power failure.
        a. Steps.
        b. Sequence.
    3. Emergency (crash) shutdown.
        a. Steps.
        b. Sequence.
        c. Securing after emergency shutdown.

A few examples to illustrate these points follow.

EXAMPLES

Radio Shack's little Owner's Manual covering their ET-275 Trim-Fone™ telephone, which has a built-in amplifier circuit, offers operating instructions that list five functions under the heading "Operation."

Another heading, "Care and Maintenance," offers a brief paragraph and checklist for maintenance, suggesting that the owner bring the unit back to the store if the checklist does not help straighten the problem out.

Equally simple is the guidance for a Sears vacuum cleaner, where the "Operating Instructions" section of the four-page manual offers only the obvious instructions to plug the cord into an outlet, turn the switch on and off, and store the vacuum cleaner with the handle upright. Maintenance instructions are confined to replacement of the bag.

The entire manual for the Sony SL-250 Video Cassette Recorder is titled *Operating Instructions*, although those instructions are only part of the content, which includes installation, maintenance, and safety instructions, along with a set of technical specifications that would probably be rather meaningless (not to mention useless) to the lay owner. The operating instructions for this item are complex and would be difficult to memorize quickly, making this a manual that most owners would be likely to want to keep near at hand for reference. The manual does make excellent use of line drawings, with some coverage by photograph also, to support operating instructions, as exemplified in Figure 7–1.

Another example of good graphics used to make operating instructions easy to understand is shown in Figure 7–2, part of a manual on operating a pushbutton memory (autodialing) telephone.

FIGURE 7–1   VCR Operating Instructions Illustrated

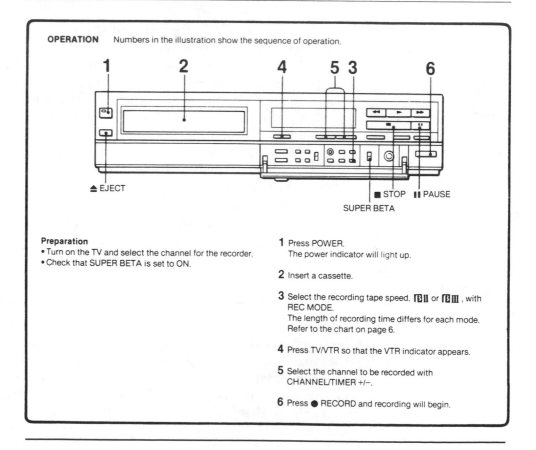

FIGURE 7–2 Telephone Operating Instructions Illustrated

LCD Display

All Segments:

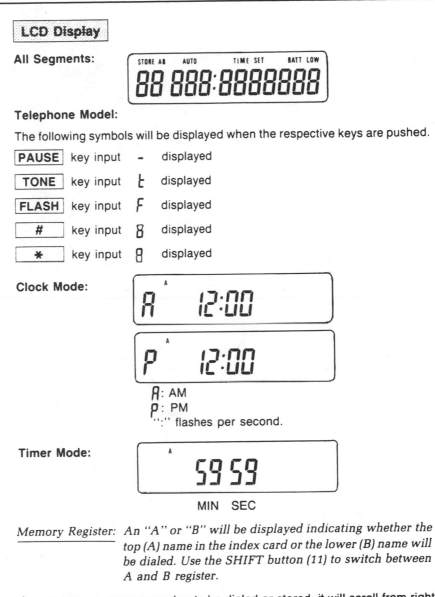

Telephone Model:

The following symbols will be displayed when the respective keys are pushed.

PAUSE	key input	-	displayed
TONE	key input	t	displayed
FLASH	key input	F	displayed
#	key input	8	displayed
*	key input	8	displayed

Clock Mode:

A: AM
P: PM
":" flashes per second.

Timer Mode:

MIN   SEC

Memory Register: *An "A" or "B" will be displayed indicating whether the top (A) name in the index card or the lower (B) name will be dialed. Use the SHIFT button (11) to switch between A and B register.*

As soon as you press a number to be dialed or stored, it will scroll from right to left on the display digit by digit. The last twelve entries will be displayed when you are through dialing.

Chapter 8

Maintenance Instructions

User instructions for maintenance are, paradoxically, the least important documentation at one end of the spectrum of user documentation needs and undeniably the most important documentation at the other end.

MAINTENANCE IS A MULTILEVEL PROPOSITION

Maintenance is nearly always an activity that operates at two levels and sometimes more than two. In today's high-tech world, the word *maintenance* tends to conjure up visions of mechanical and electrical/electronic work—trouble shooting, adjustments, and replacements of defective or worn-out parts. The fact is, however, maintenance is the act or process of keeping all things in good and usable condition, and is a need that applies to virtually everything. The most common household items—kitchen floor tiles, can openers, and dining room tables—must be maintained by cleaning, polishing, lubricating, and adjusting, as well as by trouble shooting, repair, and replacement.

At the other extreme is the maintenance of complex equipment and systems, such as a modern automobile. Maintenance, as applied to equipment and systems of this level of complexity, has an entirely different connotation, if not an entirely different meaning.

In general, all maintenance is carried out at one or both of two basic levels—preventive and corrective. Often, each of these (especially corrective maintenance) is subdivided again into levels and categories. Those several levels of maintenance are reflected in several levels of user maintenance documentation for systems where such multi-level maintenance is appropriate.

Even in terms of the maintenance of rather simple consumer items—a toaster or radio—the need for bilevel maintenance is usually recognized in the instructions to the user. An electric fan, for example, is accompanied by clearly identified maintenance instructions. They include cleaning the fan, storing it, and exercising care to avoid permitting water to drip into the motor housing, and other such do's and don'ts. To handle maintenance problems that do not respond to first-aid measures, the user is advised, the fan must be returned to the manufacturer for service.

First-aid maintenance performed by the user and true repair work performed by the manufacturer or a manufacturer-approved service station is a common bilevel approach to the maintenance of consumer items. It represents the equivalent of what the military call "echelon 1" and "echelon 2" maintenance, although the military often go to at least one additional echelon for total overhaul and repair (O&R) of many kinds of equipment. It might also be compared to what are called in military and other large organizations field maintenance and depot maintenance, respectively.

A similar approach is followed in the user manual for the Sears Craftsman Cordless Screwdriver, despite its use of several excellent line drawings, including an illustrated parts breakdown and list of parts. Maintenance instructions are brief and cursory, dwelling primarily on the "don'ts" of avoiding harmful cleaning substances that might attack plastic and/or other elements. A notice appears prominently in a box on the illustrated parts-breakdown drawing, stating that "To assure product safety and reliability, repairs, maintenance, and adjustment should be performed by Sears Service Centers or other qualified service organizations. . . ."

On the other hand, the maintenance instructions for the Black & Decker 6" Belt and 10" Disc Sander are relatively voluminous and include, in addition to the typical housekeeping or preventive-maintenance instructions, a trouble-shooting table. (See Figure 8–1.) Despite this, a typical notice is included that urges the user to have maintenance and repairs accomplished by the manufacturer or other approved qualified service station.

SUBDIVISIONS

Both general levels of maintenance (preventive and corrective) must be subdivided for more complex items. Perhaps the easiest way to clarify this and show the inevitable logic of it is to use the common automobile as an example, since most of us are quite familiar with at least the preventive-maintenance requirements of an automobile.

Preventive Maintenance Levels

Some automobile owners personally carry out certain preventive maintenance while many rely on technicians and other automobile service specialists. However, for purposes of illustration this discussion will break preventive maintenance tasks down into those that could be eas-

FIGURE 8 – 1 Maintenance Instructions for 6″ Belt and 10″ Disc Sander

HINTS TO BETTER SANDING

1. Read and understand this manual thoroughly. Follow correct assembly procedures. Give careful consideration to safety rules. **NOTE:** Maximum gap is 1/16″ between the work table and the belt or disc.
2. Hold the work firmly so that it will not be pulled from your hands.
3. Sand with the direction of the grain where possible.
4. Have different grit belts and discs available—Use rough sanding abrasives for heavy stock removal and repeat with finer grits for finer finish, consult "Recommended Accessories".
5. Move the work—holding it too long in one spot will heat up the belt and the work piece. Sometimes it can heat up enough to shorten belt life and burn the work.
6. Feed the work with light pressure. Let the grit cut and remove the stock. A heavy feed will sometimes load up the belt with dust and decrease its cutting efficiency.

Heavy feed also causes excess friction and drag which can result in motor fatigue, belt wear, possible kickback, and overall poor results.

Maintenance

WARNING: FOR YOUR OWN SAFETY, TURN SWITCH "OFF" AND REMOVE PLUG FROM POWER SOURCE OUTLET BEFORE ADJUSTING, MAINTAINING, OR LUBRICATING YOUR BELT SANDER.

If power cord is worn or cut, or damaged in any way, have it replaced immediately.

Frequently blow out any dust that may accumulate inside the motor.

A coat of automobile-type wax applied to the work table will help prevent rust and make it a little easier to feed the work while finishing. DO NOT APPLY WAX TO THE BELT TABLE because the belt could pick up wax and deposit it on the pulleys, causing the belt to slip.

WARNING: DO NOT ATTACH A VACUUM CLEANING DEVICE WHEN FINISHING IRON OR STEEL. THE SPARKS COULD IGNITE THE DEBRIS AND CAUSE A FIRE.

LUBRICATION: The drive pulley bearings and the idler pulley bearings are SEALED BALL BEARINGS—they require no further lubrication.

Trouble Shooting

CAUTION: FOR YOUR OWN SAFETY TURN SWITCH "OFF" AND ALWAYS REMOVE PLUG FROM POWER SOURCE OUTLET BEFORE TROUBLE SHOOTING.

GENERAL

PROBLEM	PROBABLE CAUSE	SOLUTION
Machine slows down when sanding	1. V-Belt too loose	1. Increase belt tension. See Page 7
	2. Applying too much pressure to work piece	2. Ease up on pressure
	3. Too much tension on abrasive belt	3. Adjust tension. See Adjustment Section, Belt Tension
Abrasive Belt Slips	1. Not enough tension	1. Adjust tension. See Adjustment Section, Belt Tension
Abrasive Belt runs off pulleys	1. Improper Tracking	1. Adjust tracking. See Adjustment Section, Belt Tracking
	2. Not enough tension	2. Adjust tension. See Adjustment Section, Belt Tension
Wood burns while sanding	1. Abrasive disc or belt is glazed with sap or worn	1. Replace disc or belt

MOTOR

CAUTION: ALWAYS UNPLUG UNIT WHEN CHECKING ELECTRICAL CONNECTIONS.

PROBLEM	PROBABLE CAUSE	SOLUTION
Motor will not run	1. Circuit breaker (fuse) open	1. Reset circuit breaker or replace fuse
	2. Low voltage	2. Check outlet for proper voltage
	3. On-off switch	3. Replace switch
	4. Loose or broken connection in motor compartment or switch terminals	4. Check all connections in motor compartment and switch
Motor will not run and/or circuit breakers (fuses) "blow"	1. Power line overloaded with lights, appliances and other motors	1. Reduce line load
	2. Short circuit in line cord or plug	2. Inspect cord and plug for damaged insulation or shorted wires
	3. Short circuit in junction box or loose connections	3. Check all connections in motor compartment and switch
Motor starts slowly, fails to develop full power or speed and/or stalls easily	1. Power line overloaded with lights, appliances and other motors	1. Reduce line load
	2. Voltage too low	2. Check and correct if necessary any low line voltage condition
	3. Undersize wire circuit (extension cord) too long	3. Increase wire size and/or reduce length of wiring
	4. Incorrect circuit breaker (fuse) in line	4. Replace fuses or circuit breakers with proper capacity units
	5. Sanding Belt too tight	5. See Adjustment Section
	6. V Belt too tight	6. See Page 8
Motor overheated	1. Improper cooling due to restricted air circulation through motor usually caused by buildup of sawdust, etc.	1. Clean out sawdust to provide air circulation through motor

Courtesy Black & Decker, Inc.

ily accomplished by owners and those that require certain facilities and/ or specialized knowledge and skills to perform.

Preventive maintenance that owners could perform personally includes:

Car washing.
Car waxing.
Interior cleaning.
Checking and maintaining battery water level.
Checking and maintaining radiator coolant level.
Checking and maintaining oil level.
Checking and maintaining tire pressure.
Replacing burned-out fuses.
Replacing burned-out lamps.
Rotating tires for even wear.
Checking and maintaining brake-fluid level.
Checking and maintaining power-steering-fluid level.
Checking and maintaining power-brake-fluid level.
Checking and maintaining transmission fluid.

It is not necessary to personally do this; the user could see to it that the attendants at service stations check on these things. Some other kinds of preventive maintenance are beyond the average owner's ability and *must* be done by qualified mechanics, such as the original dealer's repair shop staff. This is a second subdivision or category of preventive maintenance, and includes such items as the following:

Checking brakes and replacing as necessary.
Replacing worn tires.
Changing oil.
Winterizing car.
Performing periodic tuneup (spark plugs, ignition, carburetor, etc.).
Checking shock absorbers, replacing as necessary.
General lubrication, all points.
Checking front-end alignment, adjusting/repairing as necessary.
Flushing transmission, replacing fluid.

Owner Maintenance versus Service Station Maintenance

The lines that divide the type of preventive maintenance a typical owner could perform and those done by a repair shop or service station can be arbitrary. Many owners do not feel competent or disposed to do much beyond pulling into a service station and asking to have certain things checked for them. (Service station personnel will generally not go beyond offering to check oil, radiator, and battery levels, with possibly a casual visual check of tire pressure, unless specifically requested to check other items.)

Preventive versus Corrective Maintenance

The line between preventive and corrective maintenance is not always clearly distinguishable; there are gray areas. Many of the tasks listed here as preventive maintenance might fall into the corrective-maintenance category. For example, it is preventive maintenance to have your brakes checked periodically. But it is corrective maintenance to then have them rebuilt when they have worn to a certain level, the hydraulic fluid is beginning to show signs of leakage, or other symptoms suggest that it is time to replace your brakes. It is also corrective maintenance if the brakes malfunction, compelling you to seek immediate repairs. And that applies to all the other items: The inspection or checking is preventive, but when that inspection leads to repairs, the repairs are corrective, as is all maintenance performed to correct malfunctions.

There are equally unclear distinctions between many owner-performed and service-station-performed maintenance chores. The owner who is capable of doing preventive maintenance but chooses not to do so personally, instead instructing a service station attendant or mechanic to do it, is doing owner-performed maintenance via a surrogate or agent. This is not a hairsplitting distinction, either, because it has a highly significant point: It is the rationale for including guidelines in the user instructions on preventive maintenance so that users know what should be done, whether they do it personally or have someone else do it. It is not significant whose hands do the actual work, the owner/user or someone acting at the behest of and as agent for the owner/user. It is proper user information for the owner, however the owner uses it. That means that it should be furnished as part of the user instructions.

In the case of most consumer goods, even such complex items as automobiles, user instructions normally cover only those maintenance chores that the writers considered appropriate. Those are the ones that the owners might be expected to want to know about because they could be performed by owners. The owner's manual will tell you how much oil your crankcase holds, what weight of oil is recommended, where the fuses are, and similar information, but not a great deal more. In fact, many owner's manuals are deficient in educating the owner about the item and what the manufacturer's maintenance philosophy is. Owners need to understand the maintenance philosophy and the maintenance needs of the item even if they do little or no maintenance personally. The owner needs to understand maintenance at least to know what to check or have checked and when to do so. Instructions should include "when to do so"—guidance on both periodic checks and information on trouble symptoms that should send the user in search of help from the experts.

If user manuals lack such maintenance information, satisfactory operation is left largely to chance. Hopefully, the user will sense symptoms of malfunction before disaster sets in. The lack of information on proper maintenance procedures anticipates (probably unrealistically) that the user will do regular, routine maintenance and this will prevent malfunctions—or that no serious breakdowns will ever occur. The purpose of preparing maintenance instructions is to minimize breakdowns, as well as to repair equipment that has broken down.

Unfortunately, the truly technical information is normally published in separate technical manuals intended for repair technicians. The assumption is that only technicians will have use for such information. Moreover, technical manuals often occur in sets, and a large system may easily have a library of service volumes with thousands of pages of information. Even the relatively simple Silver-Reed EXP 550 computer printer, a consumer item, includes a considerable amount of technical data in the 28-page owner's manual, supported by at least four additional service manuals for technicians and/or owners interested enough to order them. One is a general technical service manual, covering the mechanical and electrical/electronic aspects of the machine. Another is a technical service manual for the serial interface. Another is for the parallel interface. And a fourth one is a separate parts catalog. All are generously illustrated, with illustrated parts breakdowns and exploded-view drawings and together total approximately 125 pages.

If the basic user's manual does not include reasonably complete coverage of maintenance, especially preventive maintenance, and there are separate technical manuals available, the user should be aware that detailed technical manuals exist. Unfortunately, this is rarely done. To get the service manuals for the Silver-Reed printer, for example, I had to call the company to find out what was available, and then send them my order. It was not until I had made several telephone calls that I discovered the existence of service manuals and the company's willingness to sell copies to users. Manufacturers are sometimes reluctant to sell their service manuals to individuals. This is because established service stations and maintenance technicians object to the practice, believing that making technical information available to users costs them business. Thus, one helpful item in all user documentation would be a list of service manuals available, with ordering instructions.

A PREREQUISITE TO MAINTENANCE INSTRUCTIONS

Routine preventive maintenance includes inspections and operational checks to detect worn parts, abnormal signals exhibited by controls and indicators, need for lubrication, and other observable symptoms. It also includes routine cleaning, lubrication, and adjustments. This can usually be done by rote, following specific printed instructions and tabulated data. And for the most part this requires relatively little technical knowledge. In a great many cases, especially with items that are not especially complex or "state of the art" (highly advanced and sophisticated technologically), it requires only the ability to recognize and identify parts and components by their names—*relief valve, limit switch,* and *tape servo,* as called out in the service instructions.

An advanced and complex item may require a large degree of technical knowledge for routine, preventive maintenance. Corrective maintenance almost invariably requires a technician who is expert in the relevant technologies generally and in the specific item specifically. For that reason, a common prerequisite to using maintenance instructions is the knowledge of, and the ability to use, information that is sometimes titled "Theory of Operation" or "Functional Theory."

Functional theory instructions assume that the reader has a sound knowledge of the relevant sciences and/or technologies and can thus easily understand technical discussions and explanations of how the item works. The concept is that the maintenance technicians must understand how the system functions normally—how it is *designed* to function—before they can detect and understand why and how it malfunctions and diagnose the symptoms of malfunction.

Functional theory instructions are a distinct and discrete element in the hierarchy of user instructions. These may constitute a page, a chapter, or a separate manual, as do the other discrete elements. A separate chapter will follow that discusses in more detail functional theory instructions. It is first necessary to understand the connection between maintenance instructions and theory of operation instructions. Maintenance—especially troubleshooting—makes it mandatory to include theory instructions in all but the simplest of user instructions. In the latter case, a few lines of technical theory information may be provided as a direct introduction to the maintenance instructions. However, we will assume here that functional theory will be discussed and presented as a separate element.

FACTORY REBUILT OR EXCHANGE SERVICE

The coverage offered in this chapter applies to all three projected levels of maintenance, preventive or routine, corrective (with troubleshooting, which is in some cases a separate chapter or manual), and overhaul and repair or depot maintenance. Depot maintenance is essentially a military concept, applying to typical military needs. The commercial civilian equivalent is factory maintenance—where the manufacturer offers a factory rebuilt service. In the case of the Silver-Reed printer mentioned earlier, the factory would not overhaul or rebuild the entire printer. They would rebuild the main electronic subassembly, a circuit board that acted as the interface between the computer and the printer, translating the computer's electrical signals into orders to the printer's circuits.

Akin to the latter is an exchange program, wherein the approved service center or factory maintains rebuilt components or subassemblies, which are exchanged with malfunctioning subassemblies for a fee so that the user does not have to wait while his or her own subassembly is being repaired. The U.S. Postal Service established such a service at its Topeka, Kansas main supply center, rebuilding certain electronic modules for its facer-canceler mail-handling machines. And, many parts suppliers take in malfunctioning items to rebuild and sell again as rebuilt parts. (There are firms whose sole business is rebuilding items for which there is a sound "rebuilt" market.) Some of the items commonly rebuilt and sold in this manner are television picture tubes, automobile batteries, carburetors, electric motors, vacuum cleaners, sewing machines, and even entire automobile engines.

On the other hand, in the electronics world of today, mass-produced circuit boards and other subassemblies or major components are often not worth rebuilding or repairing because the labor costs for even the minimal repair service exceeds the costs of the subassembly. In that case the entire board, motor, or other component is discarded and replaced, just as a single transformer or capacitor would have been a few years ago. (They are known colloquially as "throwaways.") Nothing has really changed the nature of troubleshooting and repair; the subassemblies are treated today as simple parts. In some cases, determined principally by economics (where the boards are not throwaways), chips are mounted on the boards in sockets so that the chips are easily replaceable. In some cases the entire board, with its chip population, is a throwaway; in other cases it is the bare board itself that is a throwaway: the chips are removed and plugged into their sockets on the replacement board. The chips themselves are, in practical terms, only parts—unrepairable parts—despite the fact that they are complete and complex circuits of microscopic sizes. Similar considerations apply to many other parts. (The solid-state technology of transistors and chips, with its lowered voltages and currents, resulted in the miniaturization and simplification of many other parts, such as transformers, solenoids, switches, and relays, some of which are also throwaways.)

SCOPE OF SUGGESTED OUTLINE

Maintenance instructions are often printed as three or four separate chapters or manuals—even five, in cases where parts lists are included as a separate element. All will be presented in a single outline here—again to be adapted and modified as necessary. The discrete divisions into the four elements enumerated will be shown clearly by the major heads dividing the outline into parts. The reader will normally be a technician who is properly qualified for the level of maintenance in question, by virtue of general technical training and indoctrination or full-scale training. The outline describes information that will be needed by those responsible for the management of maintenance operations, as well as those who must actually perform the maintenance personally or via personnel directly supervised by the reader.

    I.   General maintenance philosophy.
        A.   Levels of maintenance defined and discussed briefly.
            1. User or field level.
            2. Preventive/routine.
            3. Corrective.
            4. Overhaul and repair.

B. Troubleshooting considerations.
   1. Repairable versus throwaway parts.
   2. Troubleshooting aids supplied and identified.
      a. Drawings.
      b. Charts and tables.
      c. Checklist.
C. Maintenance history (if one exists).
   1. On earlier models/manufacturing runs.
   2. On similar items.
   3. On major components, assemblies.
D. Maintenance projections.
   1. Engineering tests/measurements/estimates.
      a. Reliability (MTBF).
      b. Maintainability/repairability (MTTR).
   2. Other estimates.
   3. Recommended spare parts inventory.

II. Preventive/routine maintenance.
A. Introductory instructions.
   1. General procedures and philosophy of preventive maintenance.
   2. Steps to be taken—e.g., reporting and/or replacements of parts.
B. Scheduled periodic inspection.
   1. Belts, wheels, pulleys, gears, safety interlocks, emergency controls, per drawings and charts.
      a. For wear.
      b. For irregular operation.
      c. For dirt.
      d. For lubrication.
   2. Meters, lamps, LEDs, LCDs, other indicators.
      a. For normal/abnormal indications.
      b. For operating condition of the indicator.
   3. Switches and controls.
      a. For operability.
      b. For wear.
      c. For dirt, lubrication.
C. Scheduled periodic cleaning and lubrication.
   1. Cleaning.
      a. General.
      b. All lamps and indicators.
      c. All exposed moving/bearing surfaces.
   2. Lubrication.
      a. All gears, bearings, other moving parts, per schedule.
      b. Hinges, locks, interlocks.

III. Corrective maintenance.
A. Introductory instructions.
   1. General procedures and philosophy of corrective maintenance.

          2. Steps to be taken: troubleshooting, analysis, repair and replacements, records and reports.

     B. Preliminary diagnosis.

          1. Gather symptom descriptions.

               a. By interviews with operator, other observers.

               b. By personal observation.

               c. By tests and measurements.

                    (1) Reference to engineering drawings.

                    (2) Reference to charts and tables.

          2. Read maintenance history/reports of item, if available.

               a. Most recent routine preventive maintenance.

               b. Prior breakdowns/malfunctions.

               c. Prior parts replacements.

          3. Carry out repairs/replacements.

          4. Test for normal operation.

          5. Write report, update item maintenance record.

 IV. Overhaul and repair.

     A. Introductory instruction.

          1. General procedures and philosophy of overhaul and repair.

          2. Steps to be taken: cleaning, replacements of parts, rebuilding, adjustment.

          3. Basis for overhaul and repair: reports/requests submitted by other maintenance echelons.

          4. Drawings, charts, tabular data identified and invoked.

     B. First steps.

          1. Study records of earlier maintenance.

          2. Operate item (if operable), make observations/tests.

          3. Inspect item thoroughly.

          4. Make preliminary diagnosis of extent of overhaul and repair required (unless O&R is standardized).

     C. Procedures.

          1. Disassembly, per drawings/charts supplied and identified.

          2. Inspect all parts, subassemblies.

          3. Determine which repairable, which to be discarded.

          4. Repair/replace per drawings, charts, standard procedures.

          5. Reassembly, per charts, drawings, procedures prescribed.

          6. Make all final tests for proper functioning.

  V. Parts and provisioning.

     A. Illustrations.

          1. Illustrated parts breakdowns.

          2. Exploded views.

          3. Callouts on drawings.

          4. Assembly drawings.

     B. Parts lists.

          1. Part names and numbers.

          2. Recommended spare-parts inventory.

          3. Typical (other) sources.

WARRANTIES

Some manufacturers—not all—imprint a warranty in their manuals. Two warranty statements taken from manuals are reproduced in Figure 8–2. Much more commonly, manufacturers furnish the buyer a separate form that includes their warranty and owner instructions for registering the purchase with the factory to implement the warranty.

Warranties vary widely. The warranties shown in the figure warrant replacement of the item warranted if it proves defective. The other

FIGURE 8–2 Typical Warranty Statements

WARRANTY

FOREMOST FURNITURE guarantees you, the purchaser, a complete "ready to assemble" unit. Should there be missing, defective, damaged parts, replacements will be sent to you no charge by completing and returning the enclosed part request form. To insure proper replacement of parts, this form must be returned to us at:

**FORE-CRAFT DIVISION
P.O. Box 235
Archbold, Ohio 43502**

Commercial/Industrial Use Warranty
(A Full One Year Warranty)

Black & Decker (U.S.) Inc. warrants this product for one year from date of purchase. We will repair without charge, any defects due to faulty material or workmanship. Please return the complete unit, transportation prepaid, to any Black & Decker Service Center or Authorized Service Station, listed under "Tools Electric" in the yellow pages. This warranty does not apply to accessories or damage caused where repairs have been made or attempted by others.

Like most Black & Decker tools, your 6″ Belt and 10″ Disc Sander are listed by Underwriters' Laboratories to ensure that it meets stringent safety requirements.

 This symbol on the nameplate means the product is listed by Underwriters' Laboratories, Inc.

notice, issued by Radio Shack® to cover one of its telephones, exempts instruments damaged by Acts of God, improper maintenance, or misuse. Sony® also issues a *Limited Warranty* on its VCR, limiting the warranty's time and extent. Warranty requirements vary from one state to another, so it is not possible to be completely explicit about the terms and conditions.

One factor to bear in mind in prescribing maintenance procedures and measures (and, to some extent, even in prescribing procedures and measures for other purposes) is the set of terms and conditions stipulated in your warranty. Presumably, if your product is assembled, installed, operated, and/or maintained according to your published instructions, the user has recourse if and when the item fails within the warranty period. All procedures, but especially maintenance procedures, should therefore be developed with full consciousness of these considerations and how they may affect your legal position should warranty claims arise.

There is also the matter of product liability, a subject of some importance and one that is of concern to the federal government via its Product Safety Commission.

Chapter 9

Functional Theory

The user must know and understand the functions of the item if he or she is to recognize the malfunctions and so to operate and maintain the item properly.

HOW MUCH FUNCTIONAL THEORY IS NECESSARY?

There is not very much functional theory underlying a cordless power screwdriver. Still, Sears finds it expedient to explain in the user manual for the tool that the low RPM (revolutions per minute) is not a deficiency, but is an asset because the low rotational speed translates into high torque or turning power. That and a note or two concerning the rechargeable battery used as the power source constitute the functional theory for this tool.

One reason for the scant technical information is the simplicity of the tool. It is really a quite simple device, with a chuck or *collet* for inserting and holding different bits, a battery-powered, small DC electric motor, gears and small mechanical parts, a charging stand, and a power cord terminating in a small transformer. The parts list that accompanies the illustrated parts breakdown and exploded view identifies and describes only 17 replaceable parts. The other reason for only rudimentary technical data is that the owner is not expected to do any serious maintenance work on the tool, and therefore should not require any more information than that supplied. (Presumably there are service notes available separately, including disassembly and reassembly maintenance instructions, some slightly more elaborate functional theory and, probably, some troubleshooting suggestions.)

On the other hand, the service manuals for the Silver-Reed printer include extensive technical information—functional theory—with schematic diagrams and many other drawings. That is because (1) the Silver-Reed printer is a relatively large and complex machine, with both mechanical and electronic aspects to be learned; and (2) they are manuals designed for use by technicians, rather than by owners, and it is expected that the users of these manuals will need to know all the details, electrical, electronic, and mechanical, of the printer when they are called on to service the machine.

Functional theory—the technical how-it-works information—is primarily for whoever is responsible for or will directly service and maintain the item in question. That information should be designed to satisfy the needs of that individual vis-à-vis the maintenance requirements.

There are others who may also want to read the functional theory, although not necessarily in all the technical detail that the maintenance technicians require. Equipment operators need to have a general understanding of the functional theory to do their own jobs efficiently, and managers usually feel a need to understand the equipment or system on at least the general levels of functional theory. (In the military, the managers are the responsible officers.) In fact, that alone suggests that the functional theory include a preliminary section describing functional theory in general terms—a technical summary—that does not require in-depth technical training or extensive study to master.

LEVELS OF PRESENTATION

Technical theory of operation can be presented at many levels ranging from a broad summary for managers and others who do not need technical details to a painfully detailed level for those who may have to disassemble and overhaul the complete equipment or subassemblies that malfunction. But that is not the only reason that functional theory may be presented at more than one level. There is also the nature of what is being described—the subject of the functional theory—and how that affects decisions.

SYSTEM VERSUS EQUIPMENT MANUALS

The Black & Decker belt and disc sander is an item of equipment, and the manual written for it is properly known as an *equipment manual*. Similarly, a radar set, a missile launcher, a control computer, a control console, and numerous other items making up a system are individual items of equipment, and each merits its own manual for operation and maintenance. However, since together they constitute a *system*, there is also a need for *system manuals*. Sometimes the system is manufactured in its totality by a single manufacturer, sometimes it is manufactured by several firms and assembled by one (by far the more common situation). Someone must create the system manuals—manuals that are used to guide managers, operators, and maintenance technicians in how the *system* functions, how to operate it, and how to maintain it *as a system*.

Philosophically, system manuals respond to the same needs and follow the same course of development that equipment manuals do. There is a need for installation instructions, assembly instructions, operating instructions, functional theory, and maintenance instructions at the system level. The difference between these and their counterpart equipment manuals is the level at which the instructions cut off and refer the reader to the equipment manual. Troubleshooting procedures at the system level are designed to identify the malfunctioning item of equipment, after which the maintenance technician must turn to the proper manual for that item of equipment. Functional theory also deals with the system as a system—the relationships among the various items and how each contributes to the system operation. If a missile launcher malfunctions, troubleshooting is designed to determine whether it is the launcher itself or something that controls it (such as the radar, computer, or console) that is at fault. Once that is determined, troubleshooting and repair continue at that individual equipment level.

Actually, many modern items of equipment are systems in miniature. A television receiver, although mounted on a single chassis or in a single cabinet, is a system because it consists of several discrete subsystems. The following oversimplified list serves to illustrate the principle:

- Tuner and associated circuits, that subsystem responsible for bringing in the individual channel.
- Video subsystem, responsible for the picture information.
- Audio subsystem, responsible for sound.
- "Sync" subsystem, responsible for synchronizing the picture.
- Sweep subsystems, responsible for painting the picture on the tube.
- High voltage subsystem, responsible for lighting the picture tube.

To understand television, the learner must understand the basics of these subsystems and how such circuits normally work. That is basic electronics. Learning a given television receiver is learning where each of these subsystems is located physically in the system and how each relates to the other and to the system overall. Only by understanding these elements as subsystems is it possible to make sense of it and to troubleshoot it when the system has a malfunction. A detailed drawing of a complete system, even if it is a single item of equipment with numerous functions, is almost incomprehensible to a nonexpert. Even experts would be confused, however, if they did not perceive such a drawing as a set of subsystems. A television schematic diagram, for example, is a bewildering array if viewed as other than a set of subsystems. The expert trouble-shooter views that array of circuits roughly as depicted in Figure 9–1, a rough example of a block diagram, one that shows major functions, rather than detailed accuracy. (That comes later, when examining the individual subsystems and their functioning.) Most symptoms of malfunction could be caused by malfunctions in more than one of these subsystems, so the functional theory must assist the user in troubleshooting the symptoms and identifying the subsystem that is at fault.

For this reason, block diagrams are used freely in explaining both systems and the larger and more complex individual equipment items. They help the reader understand the equipment as a set of subsystems that work together, and that in turn helps the reader perceive the logic of the troubleshooting procedures.

The shapes of the boxes in this drawing are of no particular significance; they could easily be plain rectangles, since it is only the words

FIGURE 9–1 Diagram of TV Stages

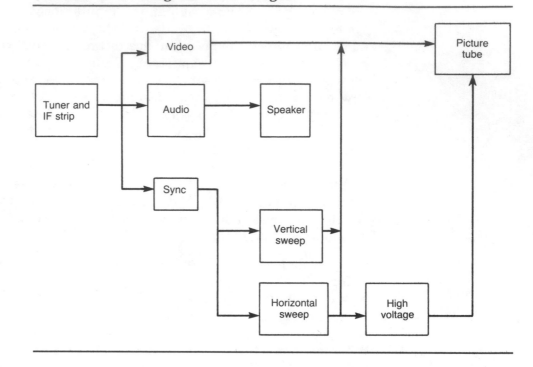

in the boxes that carry information here. In other types of diagrams, such as those drawn by computer programmers, the shape of the box helps the reader determine at a glance, before reading the words in the box, what kind of function or output is being depicted.

A COMMON ERROR

Probably the most common error made in writing functional theory manuals is the result of failing to understand the reader and what the reader needs in the way of information. Many manuals go leagues deep into technical detail—often engineering data—that is of no possible use to the reader. Other manuals offer too little technical information. I have heard an engineering reviewer object many times to the inclusion of certain details with the comment, "Aw, they'll know that," that I began to wonder why we were writing the manual at all! Equally at fault is the tendency of some technical writers to reveal everything they know about the item and the related technologies.

In more formal terms, determining who the reader is, to what use the manual(s) will be put, and the needs of the readers in that connection are known more formally as *needs assessment*. That subject will be taken up in the next chapter, along with guidelines for carrying out such an assessment and designing an efficient system of documentation.

APPROACHES TO WRITING FUNCTIONAL THEORY

Functional theory documentation is the most difficult to write because it is tutorial, as well as documentary. Assembly, installation, and even maintenance tend to follow some fairly obvious progression, often dictated by simple logic, such as the impossibility of assembling or installing something in a way that is mandated by the characteristics or design of the item. But the logical order of presentation is often not at all obvious when explaining functions and technical theory. Consider, for example, Figure 9–1 again. What is the natural order of explanation there? With so many concurrent events—many more, in fact, than are reflected in that simple block diagram—there may well be no single best way to present the functional theory explanations. Finding the best way often depends heavily on *empathy*, the ability of both the designer and the writer to perceive the reader clearly and understand the reader's probable orientation and problems. But it also depends partly on a good understanding of who the reader is and the reader's needs, as will be discussed in the chapter on needs assessment.

The functional theory manual will include information of interest and use for every user, whether assembler, installer, operator, maintenance technician, or manager. But the maintenance technician will normally require the greatest amount of technical detail. Functional theory must therefore be written to satisfy the greatest need, but the least need should not be neglected either. It may have its own peculiar requirements and may not always be satisfied automatically by writing to the greatest need.

There is also the question of the best order of presentation, and there are several possibilities for functional-theory manuals. In some cases, the best order of presentation is suggested by the nature of the equipment or system. A system in which there is a straight flow of events may possibly be best explained as a flow process, beginning with the input and tracing the flow to its output. In some cases, the reverse makes more sense, tracing the output back to its source. The reader's prior training is always a factor. If the reader is already familiar with such systems or has undergone general technical training before being trained in the specific system, a relatively high level may be used because the reader should not need painstaking detail. When ordering technical documentation for training maintenance technicians in their bulk mail centers, for example, the Postal Service specified that the trainees were recent graduates of the Postal Service's technical training courses. A profile of their prior training was an important factor in the design of documentation materials for the hands-on, on-the-job-training that followed their classroom experiences.

The nature of the equipment dictates approaches too, for maintenance need be only down to the smallest replaceable part. It is senseless to devote unnecessary time and effort to train users below that level. If the item uses typical multicircuit chips, there is no point in addressing functions below the level of the chips. Similarly, if the maintenance philosophy is to replace electric motors that fail, there is no point in teaching electric motor functional theory beyond that needed to diagnose a failed motor. (Presumably, the readers of the functional theory documentation will be technicians thoroughly trained in the basics of the relevant technologies.)

SUGGESTED OUTLINE

The approach to design of functional theory documentation is even more open ended than it is for other manuals. Therefore, as with earlier suggested outlines, it is appropriate to treat the suggested outline as a rough model that probably must be modified in adapting it to your needs. The following outline is quite general and relatively brief, in an effort to make it useful for the greatest number and widest variety of applications. That does not suggest that the functional theory manual or chapter must be equally brief; it should be designed to do its job, whatever that is and however many pages it requires. We will have more to say about both design and writing of all the manuals or chapters.

    I.   Introduction.
        A. Summary of equipment or system.
            1. Its proper name.
            2. Its basic nature, characteristics, purpose.
            3. Principal subsystems or subassemblies.
            4. Noteworthy features.
        B. This manual.
            1. Summary of its contents.
            2. Overall purpose.
            3. Organization and content.
            4. Suggested uses.
            5. Standard-nomenclature list.
            6. Cross-references to other, related manuals.
   II. Overview.
        A. System-level description.
            1. Block diagram of major subsystems/subassemblies and their functions.
            2. Walk-through by phases and major functions.
            3. Identification by nomenclature of major subsystems/subassemblies.
        B. Safety notes.
  III. Detailed discussions of each subsystem/subassembly.
        A. Signal flows and/or functional sequences.
            1. Primary function.
               a. What it is.
               b. What it does.
               c. How it does it.

2. Secondary function.
   a. What it is.
   b. What it does.
   c. How it does it.
3. Support function.
   a. What it is.
   b. What it does.
   c. How it does it.

Chapter 10

The Development of Training Manuals

Training, of one sort or another, is inevitably what user instructions are all about.

WHY TRAINING MANUALS?

User manuals are used for reference purposes, especially when they are used to document large and complex systems where reference materials are needed on a long-term, even permanent, basis. But they are also training manuals because their chief purpose is inevitably instruction—self-instruction. Users may undergo formal training in classroom, laboratory, shop, and/or on-the-job training sessions, and for these situations, the user manuals are generally used as texts to support the formal training. But they are also often supplemented with one or more special manuals designed especially for the formal training. In this chapter, therefore, we will look at some principles for writing training materials in general, especially those designed for self-instruction. We will also look at the kinds of manuals designed specifically to support formal training sessions.

THE MOST FUNDAMENTAL TRAINING PRINCIPLE

In modern times most psychologists have become behaviorists, and that concept has had a profound influence among those who conceive, develop, and/or deliver education and training materials. We will not explore behaviorism in depth; that would be far beyond the scope of this book. But it is important to understand the underlying concept, since you are almost certain to encounter the term when developing training manuals. Before exploring the meaning of *behaviorism* in connection with education and training, let's clarify the distinction between *education* and *training*.

Education versus Training

Education refers to imparting and gaining general knowledge over a wide variety of subjects and activities—language, mathematics, history, sciences, humanities, and other studies designed to prepare the individual for more advanced studies and for a productive life. *Training* is more narrowly focused on a given vocation, skill, or set of tasks, such as those discussed here. We are discussing training, not education, in these pages. Yet, basic principles are common to both—the goal of shaping behavior is a guiding principle in both—and the distinction is made here to make it clear that we are concerned only with imparting that knowledge that I have defined as training.

Defining *Behavior*

Behavior, as the behaviorist in psychology and training technology uses the term, is not *deportment,* although some people confuse the two terms. Behavior is what an individual *does,* and in training technology it is the measure of learning—the only possible measure. The rationale for this is quite direct: There is no way to determine with any certainty what an individual has learned except by observing—and measuring— what the individual does (the behavior) after the learning exposure. There is no way to determine that an individual has learned to use a hammer properly after being instructed, except to observe the individual using the hammer. The observer must be expert enough to judge accurately how well the individual is using the hammer—to rate or grade the performance. If not personally expert, the observer must be furnished with some criteria on which to base a judgment of how well the learner demonstrates that mastery or learning.

There is nothing very radical about this. Every test administered to a student is an effort to measure the effectiveness of the individual's learning by observing behavior—how well the learner does in undergoing the test, although we never before used the word *behavior* or its associated rationale. One thing that is new, however, is the concept of shaping *behavior* as the proper means of planning training programs and training-materials development by observation of what the learner does. That has led to the idea of developing and using *behavioral objectives*—objectives based on observable actions—in developing training materials.

The Behavioral Objective

The concept of a behavioral objective is simply this: The objectives of any training program and/or training materials should be stated in the precise and specific terms of the desired behavior to be achieved, rather than in the classical imprecise and unspecific terms of learning objectives couched in general terms. That is, instead of an objective that says the individual "shall learn the use of a voltmeter," it would say that the individual "shall apply the test leads to a circuit and measure voltage, current, and resistance with 100 percent accuracy." (Actually, the purists would have the behavioral description even more laboriously precise.)

Ideally, the entire training program would be planned by writing up sets of such objectives, written in even smaller increments of behavior and with much more highly detailed descriptions of qualitative and quantitative goals—measures. In fact, it is impracticably costly to carry this to the logical extreme, as experience has shown quite clearly. But the principle is a most useful one in planning and in guiding design and editorial processes. This explanation is to help you understand this most useful principle of behavior, in the special sense it is used here, to develop and write user instructions. Using this as a guide will help you in establishing valid objectives and designing effective materials.

THE PRACTICAL APPLICATION OF BEHAVIORAL OBJECTIVES

It is impractical, in terms of total effort and cost, to develop lengthy strings of objectives describing each small desired action of the learner. It is practical to be guided generally by the philosophy of thinking and planning in terms of observable and measurable behaviors. What this means is that in all phases and steps of planning, designing, and writing user instructions, you must think of what you want the user to be able to *do* as a result of your instructions. You must think of it in terms of many tasks and chores, and not just the job overall. It is that latter idea that proves unsatisfactory in achieving consistently good results. When writing a set of instructions to accompany a ceiling fan you might be addressing an objective stated most generally: the user shall be able to assemble, install, and operate the fan. However, there is an entire series of tasks or abilities—training technologists would call them *skills*—required for assembling and installing the fan. Here are a few of the abilities/skills necessary for assembly and installation:

Read mechanical and electrical drawings.
Recognize, select, and use appropriate hand tools.
Recognize each fan part or component listed and described.
Recognize each part of old ceiling fixture as named.
Turn off electricity at fuse or circuit-breaker panel.
Disconnect old ceiling fixture.
Disassemble old ceiling fixture.
Install strap for hanging fan from junction box.
Make partial assembly of motor and ball.
Hang partially assembled fan.
Make electrical connections correctly.
Install fan blades.
Install light package.
Complete assembly.
Check and test.

These abilities and tasks are only a summary of those required, but they illustrate the objectives of the manual: The user must be able to do each of these things, and each must be addressed individually as an objective. Therein lies the difference: formulating, stating, and addressing *each objective individually* to do what is necessary to satisfy each one individually.

THE PROCESS

To develop user manuals in an orderly and methodical way, an orderly and methodical process of planning is required. The process includes first a task analysis—an objective analysis of what is required for the task. It should result in a list such as that offered to describe the assembly and installation of a ceiling fan.

Task Analysis

Task analysis ought to be done or critically reviewed by someone who has actually carried out or performed the tasks and functions to be described. This is a case where there is the apparent anomaly that being too expert in the subject is often a crippling disadvantage. That is because the analysis must be carried out or reviewed by someone who is able to understand—empathize with—the user for whom the manual is intended. This is especially important when the user is a layperson. Often the writer takes for granted certain knowledge and abilities the user does not possess. Task analysis is therefore a critically important part of the planning process generally and the design process particularly. It is an especially important guide to the identification of required content and writing style. It is where and how you determine many important factors. You should, in making a task analysis, establish at least the following base data:

- A reasonably detailed profile of the reader (user), in terms of familiarity with subject of manual and/or relevant skills.
- Tools, equipment, and/or materials required.
- Whether you do or do not have to help the reader recognize and have ready ordinary hand tools, equipment, and/or materials that a technician would normally be expected to have readily at hand.
- Whether special tools, equipment, and/or materials are needed and, if so, what they are.
- Optimal sequence(s) and procedures (of assembly, subassembly, disassembly, installation, maintenance, start-up, etc.).
- Major drawings required.
- Potential hazards that must be covered as safety precautions.

For a small project in which all subjects will be covered in a single manual, a single task analysis should cover all. In a large project that can be anticipated in advance that several manuals and possibly special, formal training will be required, there ought to be a general task analysis for the project overall to define the users and the manuals required. That should be followed by a more detailed task analysis for each manual.

The data collected for each manual should be complete enough to furnish an outline that identifies all key subjects (major chapters/manuals) and main procedures for each, with notations of any and all special conditions, situations, and needs. This outline should identify all the major topics and major points to be made in the manual. Editing, revisions, and rewriting are not ruled out—far from it. Task analysis is based on early or preliminary research, and it is obviously rarely possible to anticipate everything and to plan to the last detail. However, the more effectively the task analysis is carried out, the more rapidly the writing will be completed and the less rewriting that will be required. It is a serious mistake to delay writing too long in favor of overly prolonged research and note-making. But it is an equally grave error to begin writing too soon—before conducting enough research and task analysis to have a clear understanding of what is needed and how it should be organized. Remember always that competent editors can always correct weaknesses in using language and even correct minor flaws of organization. Editors cannot repair serious errors of organization, and certainly they cannot furnish missing information or correct inaccurate information.

SPECIAL TRAINING MANUALS

All of this is valid for the development of user instructions and manuals generally, whether formal training is contemplated or not. I noted earlier that such manuals are usually employed as the texts for any formal or special training programs. However, even when the general user manuals are to be used as texts, special manuals are often required.

There are several kinds of special training manuals that can be developed to support formal training, including:

- Student manual.
- Instructor's manual.
- Administrative guide.
- Lecture guide.

No training program requires all of these. If there is an instructor's manual, for example, there may be no need for a lecture guide. An instructor's manual may also include the administrative information. The principal information to be included in the various manuals will generally include such items as those described in the following paragraphs.

Student Manual

The student manual is a guide to study and use of the general manuals that support the training. A maintenance technician undergoing special training would probably have the maintenance manual(s) and the functional theory manual as study and reference texts. The student manual would ordinarily include such material as this:

- Course outline.
- Preview/summary of course content.
- List of texts, classroom/lecture sessions, lab sessions, others.
- Schedules.
- Preview of tests to be administered.
- Study suggestions.

Instructor's Manual

The instructor's manual usually includes both specific information and guidelines and general suggestions for presenting and managing the training program. It generally includes the following, and may include some or all of the content listed for the other two special training manuals, as shown here:

- Course outline.
- Statement of training philosophy upon which course design is based.
- List of texts, classroom/lecture sessions, lab sessions, other sessions.
- Lists and descriptions of materials required and to be provided, such as audiovisual material, posters, flip charts, blackboard, other.
- Schedules.
- Suggestions and recommendations.
- Lecture notes or, in some cases, complete lecture texts.
- Copies of tests to be administered.
- Test-answer sheets or scoring keys.
- Record-keeping instructions.

Administrative Guide

In cases where the training is auto-instructional and requires only monitoring and administration, an administrative guide may be developed in place of an instructor's manual. Such a guide may include the following items. Note that tests and answer sheets are listed, for the administration and scoring of these are management chores. However, there are cases where no formal testing is contemplated and in that case such items would not be included.

- Course outline.
- List of texts, classroom/lecture sessions, lab sessions, other sessions.
- Lists and descriptions of materials required and to be provided, such as audiovisual material, posters, flip charts, blackboard, other.
- Schedules.
- Copies of tests to be administered.
- Test-answer sheets or scoring keys.
- Record-keeping instructions.

Lecture Guide

Lecture guidance is part of the instructional package and may be part of the instructor's manual or a separate manual supplied with, or in place of, the instructor's manual. In the case of large, formal training programs, there may be more than one instructor, but only one conducts classroom sessions and delivers lectures. It usually contains little other than the lecture notes or texts if supplied together with an instructor's manual, but may contain some additional information if it is to stand alone as an instructor's guide. Some or all of the following may appear in this manual:

- Course outline.
- List of texts, classroom/lecture sessions, lab sessions, other sessions with notations keying in and identifying lectures at appropriate places.
- Lists and descriptions of materials required and to be provided, such as audiovisual material, posters, flip charts, blackboard, other, again keyed to lectures, which are identified in each case.
- Schedules, keyed to lectures.
- Suggestions and recommendations for lecturing.
- Lecture notes and/or complete lecture texts.

NOTES ON TEST DESIGN

While it is not possible to offer here complete and detailed guidance in training design, the subject of test design is a most important one, and a summation of basic guidelines in test design is in order.

Proper test design is linked closely to the matter of identifying the desired behaviors. If the behaviors identified in the objectives are relevant, and meet the objectives of the training, then the tests should examine and measure those behaviors.

We must recognize that there are two kinds of behavior to consider, a "doing behavior" or motor skill, and a "knowing behavior" or cognitive skill. Each must be verified and measured differently: One is verified by having the learner display the relevant motor skill and evaluating the degree of proficiency, the other by having the learner display the relevant knowledge and evaluating the degree of proficiency. Measuring a motor skill proficiency requires that someone expert in the skill observe and rate the performance because almost invariably a subjective judgment is required. Evaluating cognitive learning, however, can ordinarily be done by anyone, using paper-and-pencil tests with answer sheets provided.

In the case of user manuals, there is normally no measurement or evaluation made except in two cases: where there is formal training in which the manuals are used as basic texts and reference material; and in cases where formal validation of the manuals is made before they are released for production. That is a subject worth a brief discussion.

VALIDATION

Too often that which appears to be theoretically sound proves in application to be either incorrect or impractical. A test or operating procedure, for example, does not produce the result promised by the writer or proves to be insurmountably difficult under the field conditions of actual operation. If the faulty procedure is not detected before the manual is produced and goes out to the users, it is obviously too late to do much about it, except send out an apologetic errata sheet or modification. But there may have been serious consequences resulting, in the meanwhile, from the misconceived procedure. It does not necessarily have to be an actual procedure that is at fault: Inaccurate information in general can bring about disastrous results.

To prevent or minimize such problems, procedures are validated by actual tryout in many sizable programs, especially those where effectiveness of operation and maintenance are absolutely critical. This is to verify that they are and do what they are expected to be and do, and that they are *practical* procedures under normal operating conditions and in the normal operating environment. It is thus a mistake to carry out validation tryouts in the shop or laboratory because that does not duplicate the normal operating conditions and environment; validation must be conducted under realistic conditions to represent a true validation.

First in importance to validate are procedures, those recommended routines and measures specified for assembly, installation, operating, and maintenance, especially under emergency conditions. (Emergency conditions should be simulated to test these special procedures.) However, it is also important to verify the effectiveness of the texts in delivering the information and directions accurately, clearly, and unambiguously. That validation is necessary to evaluate the *understandability* of all those procedures. That, too, is validation, equally important, and should be carried out if at all possible. For this validation to be completely effective and reliable it is equally important to create conditions as near the actual ones as possible. This means conducting the validation using individuals who are truly representative of typical users.

Validation is thus normally carried out *before production,* using copies of the draft manuscripts. And where formal training is to be administered to users, it is wise to utilize the initial training sessions as validation, thus validating the materials at virtually no additional cost! However, there are some special considerations in validation testing that do not apply to normal achievement testing.

Achievement Testing versus Validation Testing

Achievement testing is carried out to measure the learner's success in mastering the training, whether it is the acquisition of motor skills, cognitive learning, or both that is the objective of the training. Validation testing measures the learners' achievement only incidentally because the objective of validation testing is to measure the achievement of the training materials—the manuals, presentation aids, instructor effectiveness, and/or whatever else constitutes the program. Thus the validation testing must be also *diagnostic* if it is to be useful. The mere discovery that some parts of the material do not do the job is not enough; the tests must help the staff identify the cause of the failure.

Who Is the Failure: Learner or Program?

Modern educational theory holds that it is a fault of the training program more than it is a fault of the learner when the learner fails to master the materials. Obviously, this is a sometimes truth, with many exceptions; it is based on a premise that the learners are fully capable of learning, and motivated to learn. Still, it is a useful concept, especially when applied to a body of learners in the same group: If most of them do well, with only an occasional learner having problems, it is reasonable to assume that the program is at least adequate. It is also reasonable to assume that if all or most of the learners have difficulty, the program is probably faulty. The question is, where are the faults and what are they? To be truly effective, validation testing must answer those questions or, at least, provide clues to enable diagnosis and track down the problems so that they can be corrected.

Building Diagnostics into Validation Tests

There are several ways that validation tests can be inherently diagnostic through resourceful design. However, even without special design structured to trap faults in the program, some useful diagnoses, in at least a preliminary mode, can be made by merely observing patterns of results in the achievement testing of the learners. If all or most of the learners scored badly on some given item while doing well elsewhere, that item should become suspect.

That raises another question: is it the material offered concerning that item, or is it the way the item is tested that is at fault? That is, if the learner cannot work a problem correctly, was the teaching faulty, or is the test item misleading in what it asks? It is not a rare occurrence for a learner to know the material but misunderstand what the test question asks as evidence of the knowledge. Therefore, validation testing must also consider this possibility and include measures to validate the test items also!

One way to validate tests is to ask the same question in more than one way. A simple comparison then suggests strongly whether the learning or the item is at fault, while it also helps identify the best way to pose the item. In building tests it is a fairly common practice to do this, including perhaps three forms of each item in the initial tryout testing.

At the same time, the test items should be constructed and designed to help identify not only the fact and location of weaknesses in the program, but also the cause of the weaknesses. True–false questions are almost totally unsuitable because they lend themselves to guessing and it is virtually impossible to draw any really useful diagnostic conclusions from the results.

Probably the best form, in most cases, is the multiple-choice question. Multiple-choice questions are most helpful if the choices are carefully selected to provide diagnostic feedback. The usual practice in constructing multiple-choice items is to have one choice that is obviously wrong (that is, it should be obvious to the individual taking the test), another that is fairly plausible but clearly wrong, a third item that is almost but not quite correct, and a fourth item that is the correct answer. For validation testing multiple-choice items ought to be constructed to indicate what, why, and/or how the program material was misleading or misunderstood, if most of the learners miss the item. That means studying the learning material to judge how it might be misinterpreted or misunderstood and constructing a choice to reflect each such possibility. Test results will, of course, indicate if most had the same understanding or misunderstanding of the material. If most miss the question but no pattern emerges—no preponderance of answers on one of the wrong choices—the indication is that the material was more than misleading: it was totally unclear and failed to make any point clearly, even a wrong one!

Obviously, when the user instructions consist of a small brochure explaining the assembly of a simple telephone or the initial adjustment of a digital wrist watch, elaborate procedures and formal validation are beyond consideration. Still, simple, informal validation is possible and entirely practicable. I have used such methods successfully on numerous occasions. For example, I personally validated a simplified method for teaching logarithms by using my own secretary as a subject. She professed absolutely no knowledge of even the word, let alone its meaning, thus qualifying nicely as a test subject under my rules. After less than five minutes explanation she could explain logarithms, at least base-10 logarithms, quite easily and demonstrate at the blackboard that she did, indeed, understand the concept and the method.

At the least, simple validation of simple materials can be carried out informally by such methods. The only requirement is that the subject be not better qualified than the typical user. For user instructions intended for lay people, that is usually an easy goal to achieve.

■ Chapter 11

Some Principles of Instructional Writing

In a sense, perhaps all writing is instructional, but the writing of user instructions is a special case.

CLARITY AND COMMUNICATION

A great deal has been written about how to write clearly: Bookshelves in libraries and bookstores abound in titles on that subject. But there are many built-in Catch-22 anomalies in the subject. For one thing, what does "clear" mean? Clear to whom? Clear under what rules? For example, what a lawyer finds totally clear and easily understandable may be quite incomprehensible and confusing to the layperson. That which is crystalline in its clarity to an engineer may be totally opaque to a physician—but the reverse is also true. Clarity is almost entirely subjective, and most certainly not an absolute of any kind except in some specific set of conditions and circumstances.

Even so, clarity is not the sole frame of reference we use in discussing the subject of writing well. It is currently fashionable to speak of "communication," as well as—or perhaps rather than—clarity of expression. The notion of communication is a bit more concrete and helpful, but again it is only a term. The implication in using the term is that it refers to *accurate* and perhaps complete communication, but that is not assured either: The recipient does not always get the message that was sent or was intended by the sender.

The Factor of Communication

To some degree the problem lies in what constitutes *understanding*. Understanding is bound up in emotion, as well as in reason. We tend to "understand" that which we believe or wish to believe. We do not, and probably cannot, understand a law with which we strongly disagree

115

or the popularity of a public figure we happen to dislike. However, we readily understand the reasonableness and rightness of a law we agree with and the appeal of a public figure we find likable.

Writing to Persuade: The Motivation Factor

Clarity and communication are not the only issues in instructional writing. If understanding is linked closely to belief or desire to believe—perhaps even stemming from that desire—then we must learn how to write *persuasively* if we are to communicate clearly and bring about understanding. And that does prove to be a helpful idea; persuasive writing motivates readers, making them *want* to understand, with salutary results. *Motivation* is the $64 word. Motivation is magic: it has a magical effect on human behavior. A wartime infantry soldier once defined morale, when he said, "Morale is what makes your feet do what your head knows is impossible." The same could be said of motivation. Motivation is the factor that enables many people to overcome tremendous obstacles and achieve what others, even experts, consider to be impossible. The near-miraculous accomplishments of Thomas Alva Edison and Alexander Graham Bell are inspiring examples.

Persuasive writing is writing that motivates readers to accept, to understand, to *believe* what they are reading—what the author is saying. It has its greatest application in advertising and sales copy of all kinds, of course, but it is also useful to understand its principles for and their applicability to all kinds of writing.

The Chief Principle: Appeal to Self-Interest

Each of us finds our own self—our ego—our most important interest. We love to take those little self-evaluation quizzes so often published in weekly tabloids and magazines because the results supposedly reveal something about us, if nothing more than that we score highly. Astrology columns are popular for the same reason. And, writing that addresses the reader directly as "you" has far greater impact—and is far more persuasive when arguing a case—than writing that refers to "the reader" or "one." Compare the following two statements with each other to see how the simple change from "one" to "you" changes the effect:

1. One can have a more youthful skin with Purple Ointment.
2. You can have a more youthful skin with Purple Ointment.

A simple change of one word ("can" to "will") helps make the statement more persuasive, while increasing its impact also by making it a direct promise, instead of an implied one. Even that can be improved by another slight change, replacing "with" with "when you use," as witness the next two sentences:

3. You will have a more youthful skin with Purple Ointment.
4. You will have a more youthful skin when you use Purple Ointment.

But even more impact is possible. Using the imperative mood, as in the following sentence, increases impact dramatically:

5. Have a more youthful skin; use Purple Ointment!

And breaking the third sentence into two sentences increases the impact again:

6. Have a more youthful skin! Use Purple Ointment!

Now compare number 6 with number 1, and you should begin to see the effect of the words and the structures you use. In each case the appeal is to the reader's ego—self-interest—but the messages become increasingly more personal, more specific, and more imperative. And all make their contributions to believability and persuasiveness accordingly. The chief motivator is self-interest—the prospect of having a more youthful skin. The degree to which that motivates the reader depends on the power of the message: the specificity with which the promise is made and the specificity with which the reader is urged to action.

Four of the basic qualities to seek in your writing, then, are these:

- Appeal to reader's interest.
- Specificity.
- Imperative mood.
- Direct address.

Let's take a somewhat closer look at each of these. But first, a relevant observation of the examples that were used to illustrate some of the points: manuals and other user instructions are not advertising. Neither are they attempts to persuade readers to spend money, to make a donation, to vote for some candidate, or other traditional sales appeal. So such messages as "you will have a more youthful skin" are not directly applicable here. At the same time, the principle on which such a message is based is not totally irrelevant: The user instruction is trying to "sell" readers on recommended procedures and/or functional explanations. Readers of manuals and other user instructions have self-interests, and respond to appeals to those self-interests. Moreover—and this ought to be a major consideration for the seller—the reader's reaction to the instructions will color his or her opinion of the item about which the instructions are written.

What does the user of a hair-coloring preparation think of the preparation when its application turns out badly and the user's hair is colored in some garish fashion? It may be the fault of the instructions and not of the product, but the typical user will immediately condemn the product, and understandably so. That applies to other items as well. Even when the project turns out satisfactorily—the user did finally manage to assemble the bookcase, despite badly written instructions, for example—the user still has only an unpleasant association with the product and this will influence his or her overall opinion of the product and perhaps of all products of that manufacturer. (The latter result is particularly likely and especially damaging when the manufacturer is a well-known corporation that manufactures a great many well-known products.) In the end everything the seller writes and publishes for public consumption has its effect on the seller's image and marketing, and is therefore a sales message, even if only indirectly and subtly so.

APPEAL TO READER'S INTEREST

Readers have many interests, and one self-interest that applies here is the reader's comfort in reading. There is comfort in easy and pleasant reading, as compared with dull and tedious reading, a sin of which too many user instructions and their writers are guilty. If the user finds the instructions "heavy going"—dull, ponderous, and opaque—the user may have difficulty in comprehending the instructions (as well as a growing distaste for the product). The reader of dense text finds it difficult to understand, even when all necessary information is presented and in logical sequence. (Personally, I find dull movies also difficult to understand. But maybe the reverse is the case, and it is the difficult-to-understand movie that I find dull. In either case, it does not make me a champion of the movie.)

All of the four measures to be discussed here have an effect on readability of the material. I have not yet mentioned the injunctions most authors of how-to-write-well books tend to stress heavily—short sentences, short words, simple sentence structure, and similar exhortations. They will not be neglected entirely, for they are legitimate concerns and considerations, but it is my opinion that they are less important than the other factors mentioned. (I base that in part on my experience in developing manuals and in readers' reactions to my own writing, which has never tended especially to short declarative sentences and/or to short words, but does tend to the other qualities recommended.)

Aside from the sheer comfort of perusing easy-to-read and easy-to-understand materials, there is the reader's interest in finding the procedures themselves easy to implement. The ease or difficulty of carrying out the procedures stipulated may be partly inherent in the product's characteristics, but they are certainly also at least partially the result of how they are conceived and designed (possibly including the wisdom of the sequence) and partially to how they are explained.

Even the sequence can be an important factor. In installing a ceiling fan for the first time one of my difficulties was in assembling and installing the light package. The instructions were to do this last, after the fan was in place, hanging from the ceiling. I found it most awkward to do so, trying to work overhead at a fairly intricate task. (It was made more difficult also by the lack of detail on how to mount the light package on the main fan assembly.) When I installed a second ceiling fan I departed from the written instructions and installed the light package in the fan assembly before I hung the fan. It proved an immeasurably easier and more practicable sequence, and made me wonder whether anyone had tried out the installation instructions—validated them—while they were still in draft form. (The product was well made, but I was tempted to return it in sheer frustration at the difficulties resulting from poorly conceived procedures and, in at least one area, actual error in a wiring diagram.)

Using simple illustrations, preferably simple line drawings in most cases, is another important factor in making the user feel comfortable. The user has far less difficulty in identifying components, parts, tools, and procedural steps when they are illustrated, of course. Fear of the unknown is a factor, and good illustrations help greatly in making the unknown less strange.

That is itself an important point. Many users want reassurances in general, especially when they are facing an unfamiliar job which they find somewhat intimidating. Consider the layperson who is unpacking his or her new computer and must assemble, interconnect, and begin to learn how to use the several components. That user can hardly help having some trepidations and perhaps awe of what he or she may regard as an almost impossibly complex product. New users need assurances that other quite ordinary mortals learn to use the machines easily, that it is almost impossible to harm them through keyboard mistakes, and that the key to success is slow and careful following of the procedures.

The text ought to reassure the user by specifying safety precautions and procedures when they apply, but not in such manner as to alarm the user. The user should be assured that there is no danger if the precautions are observed. The extensive set of manuals provided with

FIGURE 11–1 Line Drawing of Typical Personal Computer

Basic Computer Parts

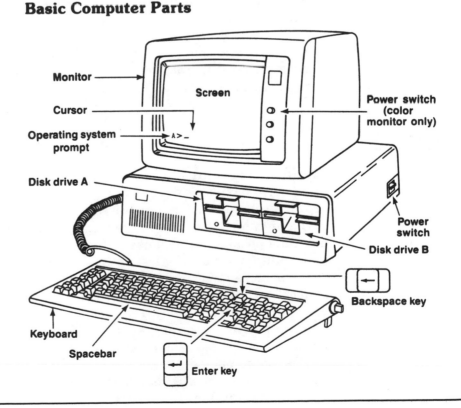

Courtesy MicroPro International Corporation

FIGURE 11–2   Illustrating How to Insert a Floppy Disk

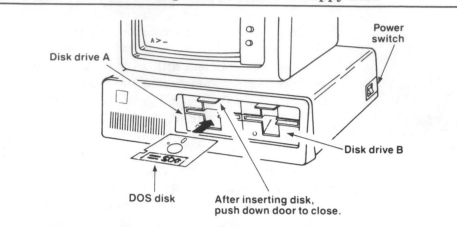

Courtesy MicroPro International Corporation

the new WordStar Professional Release 4 offers a good example of re-assurances offered users. The first manual is small one—14 pages—titled *What's New*. It begins by stating that many useful new features have been added to WordStar, but that the new program is entirely compatible with earlier WordStar editions, so that files created with earlier versions can be used with the newest edition with no difficulty. It then lists and explains each new feature and other reference material.

Wisely, instructions intended for those new to word processing are in separate sections so that old hands can skip this and go on to the instructions and information suitable for them. That section, however, addresses those new to WordStar, those new to word processing, and/or those new to computers in general, including several excellent line drawings that illustrate typical personal computers of today. (See Figures 11–1 and 11–2.)

SPECIFICITY

Specificity has a great deal to do with the user's comfort and peace of mind when facing the task of coping with whatever the user instructions are about. Vague and general discussion and directions add to the sense of the unknown and thus to the user's uncertainty and fear. Specificity has the opposite effect, making the item and the steps to be followed more familiar and thus less intimidating. However, there is another, perhaps more important, consideration: The effect of specificity on the general credibility of the instructions and on the user's sense of confidence in the instructions.

Almost anyone can generalize about almost anything without risking serious error—if the generalization is broad enough. And "broad enough" means vague enough. If an automobile mechanic estimates that your automobile repairs will be "around" or "roughly" "two to three hundred dollars," it is unlikely that you will leave your automobile to be repaired there. You would have little faith in the "estimate," (obviously not very well thought out) and you would wonder if the mechanic knew his business. The same consideration would apply to a vague diagnosis or vague promise, such as the opinion that "the problem is somewhere in the transmission" and the suggestion that you should "just leave it, and I'll take care of it, whatever it is." The credibility of the instructions and your confidence in them are in almost direct proportion to the degree of specificity—amount of detail—embodied in them.

The instructions of a device for carrying an infant in a backpack are an example. The first instruction, for disassembly of the original package, presumably (the instructions do not specify), is "Untie lacing on waist band and cord." Despite simple line drawings offered to guide the assembly, nowhere are the "lacing," "waist band," or "cord" identified. Neither are the "cross bow" and other components mentioned in succeeding instructions. However, the assembly instructions are well illustrated and the text clear enough, fortunately, so all is well after a bad start.

In many cases, user instructions depend almost entirely on detailed drawings with very little text. This is fine for some users—engineers, mechanics, and technicians—but for others—lay persons, especially—this can be disastrous when the drawings are technical diagrams and are quite "busy" with many callouts, labels, and other markings. Many laypeople will find such detailed illustrations baffling, if not formidable, and will be able to make only limited use of them. Simple drawings with good supporting text is usually a better idea.

Even when specificity and details do not have a direct bearing on the information or procedures they have a pronounced psychological effect in generating a sense of confidence in the material. For that reason, as well as because of practical benefits resulting, the following writing policies are helpful.

Always try to *quantify* by supplying numbers instead of qualitative adjectives and adverbs. "Supports at least 350 pounds" is much more specific than "Supports most adults easily." Quantitative statements are normally accepted as factual statements, whereas qualitative statements often appear to be "Hollywood" or "Madison Avenue" (and often are just that).

Avoid rounding off numbers. Use exact numbers whenever possible. At least, estimate quantities as closely as possible. "Supports an estimated 275 pounds" is far better than "Supports about 300 pounds."

Avoid hyperbole and *anything that appears to be hyperbole* in general. That means avoid scrupulously whatever appears to be an extravagant statement, rooted in superlatives, such as "most," "greatest," and "latest."

Make specific statements. "Must be anchored in concrete for stability," rather than "Tends to be unstable if not anchored firmly."

IMPERATIVE MOOD

The imperative helps inspire confidence in the instructions because it is both authoritative and reflective of the writer's own confidence in the instructions. It *directs* the reader. Rather than "Must be anchored in concrete for stability," use "Anchor in concrete for stability," as though you were issuing orders.

Many people prefer to be issued instructions in this manner and react best when the instructions are so cast in the imperative mold. They want to be told exactly what to do and how to do it, and in that direct-order form. They want to be *led*.

Of course, this applies to procedural instructions; it would not be appropriate for functional theory manuals. However, it is suitable for listing and prescribing procedures for assembly, installation, adjustments, preventive maintenance, and corrective maintenance and should be used in these manuals.

DIRECT ADDRESS

Direct address is appropriate everywhere, even in functional theory manuals and general overviews or descriptive materials. It is somewhat akin to the imperative, although not identical (although imperative mood is a form of direct address). For example, "Fifteen volts should appear at the junction of R2 and C24" is indirect, whereas "Fifteen volts appears at the junction of R2 and C24" is direct. (There are more technical terms, such as *subjunctive mood* that apply here, but this is not intended to be a grammar course.)

Indirect address is tiresome and lacks vigor, therefore lacking impact. It also suggests that the writer is not entirely sure of the facts, and that does not help inspire confidence in the instructions. I have noticed that reports written by a certain class of professionals often begin summarizing statistical material with a sentence along the lines of "This figure tends to suggest the possibility that one might expect to find at least one group that does not conform fully to the norm." This kind of hedging destroys any confidence I might otherwise have had in the conclusions the writer has drawn. How could it do otherwise? Better to say "This figure eliminates Group A from further consideration."

It is appropriate to refer to this as writing in the *positive mood*, distinguishing it from the negative mood exemplified by a statement loaded with escape clauses. For that is the crux of the matter: the inclusion of even single escape clauses, let alone multiple ones, is a confession of weakness and lack of confidence in one's material.

SHORT WORDS AND SIMPLE SENTENCES

There have been several efforts to establish methods for measuring and controlling something called *readability* of text passages. The *fog index* or *fog count* attempts to measure how difficult a given text passage is, while it also represents a method for writing to a given grade level or given level of so-called readability.

There is a computer program to help measure readability through the automation of measuring it. You can implement this by typing a sample and having the program evaluate it, but it is probably more practicable and certainly more useful to have the program measure an actual portion of your manuscript. See Chapter 14 and the Bibliography for more information about this.

The fog index overlooks the problem of what the general semanticists have referred to as one's *referents,* which is what really determines readability. A *referent* is the image or meaning invoked in an individual when he or she hears a word. In general, it refers to the individual's vocabulary, but even that is not entirely accurate. We all understand the word *automobile* or the word *chair* easily enough, but the image invoked by the words will be different in each individual, according to that individual's referent for the word. The fog index is flawed in that the method is based on a false assumption, the assumption that if sentences and words are short—the fog index measures readability by counting sentence length in words and word length in syllables—the text will be highly readable. It ignores the fact that many quite short words are completely unknown to most individuals, while many polysyllabic words are quite common and well known. So "The earth is an oblate spheroid" is not as "readable" as "The earth is shaped like an orange, round and flattened slightly at the ends," despite the sentence, word, and syllable counts that would favor the first sentence.

Other readability measures, such as the well-known Dale-Schall method, surmount this difficulty by invoking a vocabulary list for each grade level. Unfortunately, that becomes a quite laborious and impracticable method, although the personal computer may make it more practicable in the near future.

The Author's Responsibility

Whether we call it *readability* or *understandability,* achieving it is a responsibility of the author. As with learners and training programs, it should be assumed that usually when the reader has difficulty in understanding the author's intended meaning, it is the author's failure, not the reader's failure. The following discussions are based on that premise.

There has been a considerable amount of work done to help authors achieve a high degree of readability and control over readability. But superior readability and control are still achieved through the writer's and editor's art, not through a scientific method. Even the most common terms have more than one meaning, a meaning that varies with and depends on the context in which it is used and/or the individual's referent.

Denotation versus Connotation

Words have both *denotative* and *connotative* meanings or meanings that are, respectively, literal definitions and meanings that are implied shades or nuances of meaning. For example, *stubborn, obstinate,* and *determined* are synonyms in their denotation, but not in their connotation. *Stubborn* connotes an unreasonable resistance, which is a negative implication. *Determined* has a positive implication, suggesting an admirable trait. But even those shades of meaning do not necessarily always attach themselves automatically to those words; the context may suggest the opposite intended meanings of the author, as in "He was determined in his efforts to steal a great deal of money" or "Edison persisted stubbornly in his search for the right material."

Many words have more than one literal meaning. For example, many words can be used as more than one part of speech. *Barge* is both noun and verb, as are *screw* and *bolt*. *Olive* is both noun and adjective. Many words are used commonly as metaphors, where literal definition is not intended: "He was a smiling little gnome," and "She stood frozen," are examples.

Do not make assumptions as to the extensions of words and their meanings, for English is not a totally rational language, and what appear to be logical conclusions are not always correct. A good dictionary is an essential. For example, one technical writer wished to explain that the many connection terminals in an electrical-equipment cabinet had each been assigned an identifying number. He thought it logical to use a noun version of the word *assign* and so wrote of the "assignation" of terminal numbers, totally unmindful of what that word means to most of us. Another technical writer wished to advise readers that all the critical circuits in the equipment about which he was writing were "backed up" by duplicate circuits. He unhesitatingly advised readers of the "duplicity" of the circuits.

Helping Your Readers

Writers especially must develop a sense of language that enables them to judge accurately that which is most readily understood by the average reader. They should provide some means of assistance to the reader when using words or terms that are uncommon or for any reason judged likely to be unknown to many of the readers. There are two classes of such words: those that have general meanings, but are either not in everyday use or are quite commonly misunderstood (as I once discovered, to my dismay, was the word *epitome*); and those that are the technical terms or otherwise specialized jargon of the industry or craft that is the subject (or environment) of the instructions. There are two ways, to keep the reader informed as to your intended meaning when you use such words and terms.

Sentence Structure Can Be Connotative Too

Words and terms that you judge should be explained or defined for your readers are usually handled by direct definition, such as I used here in introducing the terms *denotative* and *connotative*. That can be carried out parenthetically, as in this case, or parenthetically in a more literal sense by following the word immediately with a definition enclosed in actual parentheses. Words can also be defined indirectly by arranging the context to make your intended meaning clear. The structure of the sentence "Although he was usually intractable, he could be yielding and pliable when confronted with the right arguments" should enable the average reader to infer the meaning of *intractable* without difficulty. The overall meaning of the sentence conveys this definition, and also the positional significance of the words aids the effort. The use of the word *although,* suggests that contradictory or conflicting meanings are being presented. Positional significance can do much to change the meanings, not literally, but via denotation—by making the author's intended "slant" quite clear. Consider, for example, the following two sentences, which use the same words but in different arrangements, with drastic differences in the messages:

1. Joe drinks, but he is a good worker.
2. Joe is a good worker, but he drinks.

Nomenclature

If your text contains few technical terms and little jargon, you can handle the problem of defining your terms in the same manner you help your readers understand your general words and terms. However, where you must use many such special terms that you cannot expect your readers to understand (even technical experts cannot be expected to understand the special terms that arise in connection with the development of new products), you must resort to other means. And there is a means that is something of a de facto standard in such work: The glossary and/or the nomenclature list.

The glossary and nomenclature list are not really identical, for a glossary is a general list of all special terms, while a nomenclature list is a list of the names and designators assigned to functions, equipment, parts, assemblies, subassemblies, and other components of both hardware and software belonging to the system. In practice, however, the nomenclature list is often extended so that it is a general glossary of all terms in the text that have special or uncommon meanings.

It is a wise practice—in fact, should be a mandatory practice—to define each special term carefully when it is introduced and all well-designed and well-written manuals do so. However, that is not enough, for several reasons, which we shall explore in a moment. Those reasons make it also a wise practice to include a glossary and/or nomenclature list when more than a handful of special terms appear in the text, and that too ought to be made a mandatory practice. Certainly, it will help you to avoid many problems.

The primary purpose and importance of a glossary is that it ensures clear communication by defining all terms that might not be understood by readers or at least defining them as the author wants and means them to be understood. Nomenclature lists have a somewhat broader and more diversified purpose—they establish the proper and usually official names for all items and references, especially those that are unique in the application at hand. In so doing the list satisfies more than one need:

1. It establishes or at least documents officially the proper assigned names and terms, thereby heading off the problems that inevitably arise when this is not done.
2. It furnishes for the reader a definition of each name or term.
3. It provides a ready reference for the reader to look up a term if he or she encounters it later in reading and has in the meanwhile forgotten its meaning.
4. It provides the writer(s) a consistent and uniform list of names by which to refer to parts, equipment, components, functions, and other such items.

The latter, item 4, is itself no small consideration, and is a reason for developing the nomenclature list as early in the writing project as possible. Almost invariably and inevitably, when this is not done—especially when an entire staff of writers is working on a documentation project—various items in the system come to be referred to by various names. For example, items may be referred to by both numbers and functional designators. That is, a transformer that appears on a schematic diagram as *T22* may be so referred to on one page, while it is referred to as an *output transformer* on another page, and even as the *third-stage coupling transformer* on still another page or in another chapter. The result is near-total confusion of the reader. It is essential that nomenclature be consistent. If it is necessary to refer to *T22*, the reference should include the official name of the part—for example, *"the coupling transformer (T22) . . ."* Otherwise, the confusion is inevitable. This is entirely unacceptable and results in a costly and time-consuming effort to straighten the problem out. That means a great deal of editorial work to make the necessary changes later, when the problem is discovered.

The engineering staff at Remington-Rand Univac laboratories in Blue Bell, Pennsylvania, developed the revolutionary LARC computer, and dubbed a certain set of registers in the computer "shmoo registers." The term was an allusion to characters invented by the late cartoonist Al Capp and was inspired by the result of an oscilloscope presentation in testing certain registers. The trace that appeared on the oscilloscope when making these tests resembled the shmoo characters as drawn by Capp, or at least the engineers thought it did. After the manuscript was complete and had been submitted in draft to the customer, the U.S. Navy, Navy officials reacted almost violently to the frivolity represented (at least in their minds) by the name assigned. They demanded that the name be changed to something more sober, and it was only after much time spent in meetings and discussions that the nomenclature list was amended to change "Shmoo Registers" to "Fast Registers." Extensive work was required to expunge the shmoo reference and replace it with the proper one throughout the entire set of manuals. (Today, with the manuscript in a personal computer, having been developed via a word processing program, the revision would be much simpler, although still unnecessary extra work.)

Chapter 12

Basics of In-House Publishing

Far too many writers, editors, and managers of writing and editing think that they need not be concerned with production functions. But to be an efficient part of the whole, you must understand the whole.

WHY THIS CHAPTER

In this chapter I am going to treat the *whole* of in-house publishing, especially that referred to as *production*, because I believe it is important for creative people performing creative functions to appreciate the entire process. There is another purpose. While many large corporations have large in-house publications departments staffed with expert professionals, smaller organizations usually must improvise a publications staff or vend the job to specialists who do such work. In either case, the managers of the smaller organizations can use a bit of guidance to help them with an unaccustomed task.

IN-HOUSE PUBLISHING IS NOT WHAT IT USED TO BE

In-house publishing has changed remarkably in the past few decades, very much for the better. Here is a summation of the major changes that have taken place in the short few decades of my own experience:

■ In-house composition has gone from electric typewriters—principally IBM Executive and Selectric machines—to computerized typesetting via word processing and desktop-publishing programs, using the newer 24-pin dot matrix printers and the modern laser printers. In another sense, it has gone from what was obviously "typeset" by ordinary electric typewriters to what now appears to closely rival formal, classical typesetting. Metal type has all but disappeared in favor of what is referred to now as "cold type," to distinguish it from the practice of pouring molten metals into molds to form letterpress characters.

■ In-house printing is now incredibly easy, even easier than with the automatic or semiautomatic small presses. This is particularly true for short runs (small quantities) that are so often typical of in-house publishing, using personal computers with their desktop-publishing programs and xerographic office copiers that produce copies of excellent quality that are all but indistinguishable from formally printed copies. Except for the long runs—thousands of copies—it hardly pays now to turn to the printing press.

■ Out-of-house printing has changed too, with letterpress almost as extinct as metal type, replaced by swift, easy, and inexpensive offset presses.

■ The writing process has changed, to a small degree, but not nearly enough—not nearly as much as it should. That subject will be taken up in more detail in a separate discussion on word processing.

Production

The production phase normally includes the composing of text, illustrating, making copy up into pages, printing, and binding. Printing and binding once typically vended out to a commercial printer, may be done in-house, since many organizations do have internal printing and binding facilities, and for short runs may even use an office copier for "printing" and a desktop binder, such as one using the 18- or 19-hole punch and plastic combs, or they may even "side stitch"—staple—the manuals.

Production tasks that are preliminary to printing are usually the responsibility of the art department or a production department that includes a group of illustrators. That is because most of the chores of production require the skills of the illustrators. And where there is a typing pool for the production of camera-ready text, that is quite often under the management of the production department or art department.

Final Draft May Not Be Truly Final

Although production normally follows final changes and the development of final draft, certain qualifiers must be established here. In fact, there are often several phases or even cycles of production. In the case of large projects, where as many as 200 or more copies of a final draft are needed for various purposes, it is not unusual to go through entire production processes to produce draft copies before truly final production and the full-scale printing run.

There are at least two reasons for the need of a large number of copies of the final draft—and that final draft, remember, is not the truly final manuscript. One reason is the need for evaluation and review by a large number of reviewers. A military organization may wish to send copies out to a large number of reviewers stationed in many places and solicit their comments. There is also the need for validation, which would normally be performed using copies of the final draft.

Even these are not always the truly penultimate final draft, for if there are significant problems with the draft, problems that require quite drastic and extensive revisions, it may be necessary to print several hundred copies of the revised manuscript and repeat the processes of reviews and validation tests before going to final production.

Production Is Not Absolutely Sequential

Aside from this, production is not a discrete phase that starts abruptly when the final draft is typed. Some production tasks are carried out concurrently with writing. One of these is illustrating. Many illustrations begin life as writers' rough sketches, as writers' adaptations of existing illustrations, or even as photographs that the writers wish to have adapted to the need. But many illustrations are finalized long before the text is, and so may be turned over to the illustrators for production while writing continues.

When the project is a sizable one, the manuscripts go to production in a stream, chapter by chapter or manual by manual, as work progresses. In fact, efficient planning would schedule the work in this manner in an effort to keep the workload as steady as possible and avoid the wasteful alternations of tall peaks and deep valleys of activity.

Basic Production Processes

Aside from creating and/or adapting line-drawing illustrations, the production staff performs chores to create the following:

Page layouts, rough and comprehensive.
Paste-ups and mechanicals (camera-ready pages).
Printer's dummies.
Running sheets.

Page layouts are plans that show how each page will appear—where and how headlines, captions, text, illustrations, tables, and/or other elements will appear. They are done first in rough, which are preliminary estimates of how and where the various elements will fall into place, and then, as the project progresses and it is possible to plan more precisely, *comprehensive* layouts replace the rough layouts, showing more precisely what the final pages will include.

Figures 12–1 and 12–2 illustrate this. The differences are of degree, not of kind. The second of the two figures merely shows a growing knowledge of exactly what the final product will look like.

Paste-ups and mechanicals are simply those comprehensive layouts implemented: The text has been pasted down on forms (see Figures 12–3 and 12–4), along with suitably sized copies of relevant line drawings or other line copy. If a photo is to appear on the page, a *mask* is emplaced there. This is a block of black or red paper (the camera sees red as "blacker than black") to create a *window* in the photo negative, in which will be pasted (*stripped up*) a screened negative of the photograph.

FIGURE 12–1   Rough Layout

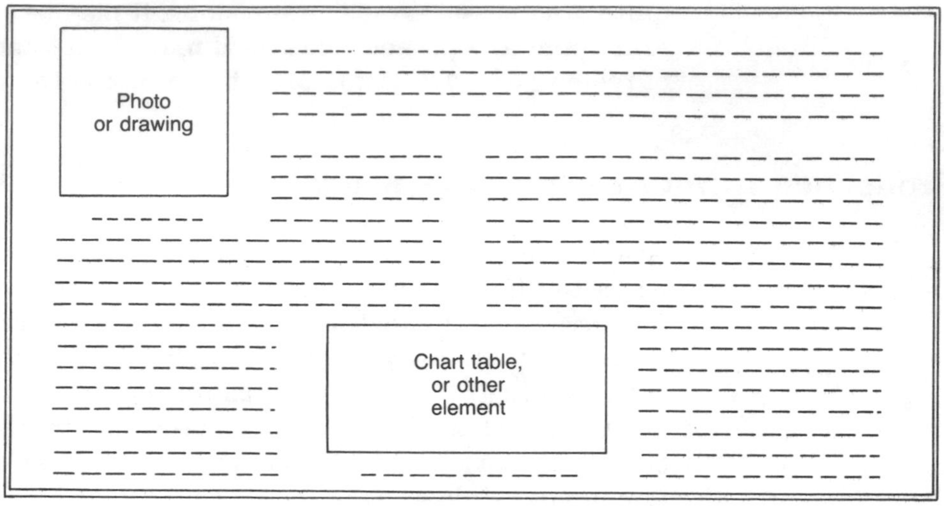

All of this is indicated in the comprehensive layout, which is the master plan or blueprint for pasting up copy, as it is completed, to become the *mechanicals* which will ultimately go to the printer.

There are several variations of this design. However, the important thing is that the markings are printed in a pale blue—sky blue—which is invisible to the camera and is thus seen as white and known as *nonreproducible blue* or, colloquially, as *non-repro*. Traditionally, copy was typed on these forms, which had guidelines for single or double-column copy and for other provisions. The paper itself was treated with various substances, such as being clay coated, to make it "whiter than

FIGURE 12–2   Comprehensive Layout

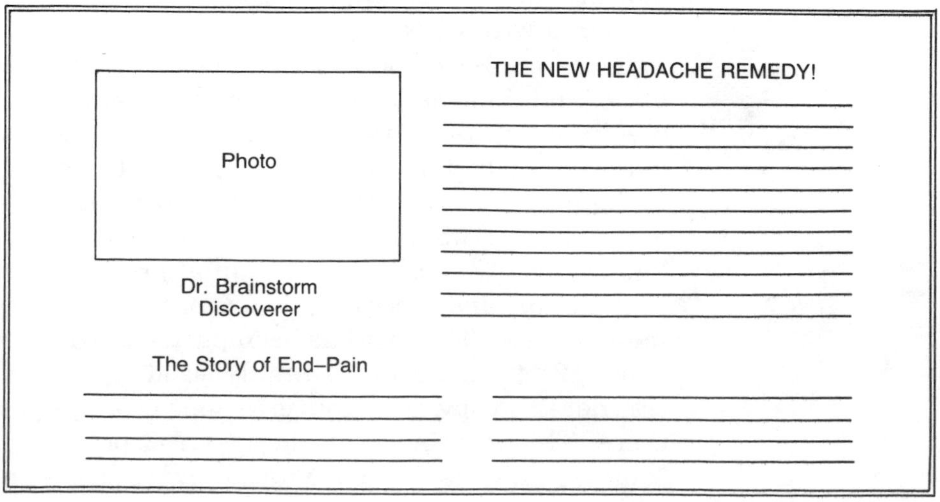

FIGURE 12-3 Typical Form for Pasting Up Type

white" and otherwise create the sharpest image possible. The printing plates are made directly from these forms, using photographic processes.

With modern and steadily improving processes and machines, it is less and less necessary to go to extremes in these matters. But much of that is reserved to the discussions to come on word processing and desktop publishing.

Photographs must be cropped: Most photographs include too much material that detracts from the main message. Therefore, production

FIGURE 12-4   Alternate Form for Pasting Up

Column 1	Column 38	Column 76

departments crop the photo to indicate that portion of the photo that is to be used and that portion that is to be deleted. The photograph is mounted on a rigid material—*art board*—and the board is marked to delineate the area of the photograph that is to be reproduced, as Figure 12-5 shows. With this method the photograph is itself untouched, except for mounting, and may be used again and again and recropped as desired.

FIGURE 12-5 Photograph Mounted and Marked for Cropping

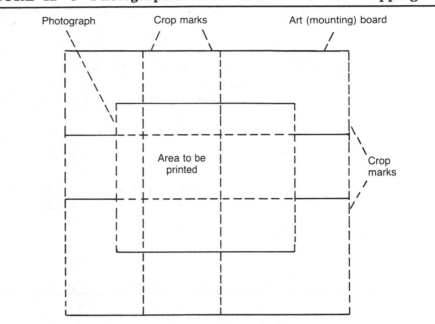

Printer's Dummies

A printer's dummy is a device to help the printer understand the sequence of pages and method of binding them. It is generally used only for small publications. It consists of plain paper folded to represent the desired end product, with pages numbered. For a larger publication it is usually more practical to make up something called a *running sheet,* which serves the same purpose. To understand that more fully, it is necessary to point out some typical practices in generating user manuals.

In fact, in many technical-publications programs layouts are not used at all because certain popular expedients (some of them dictated by military specifications for technical manuals) make them unnecessary.

A FEW TYPICAL PROBLEMS AND THEIR SOLUTIONS

Determining where illustrations, tables, and other nontext elements will occur in the document is always a problem, and is also a waste when there are to be two or more production cycles to accommodate the need for extensive reviews and validation tests. To avoid this expense, certain expedients have become fairly common practice: every illustration, table, or other nontext element is allotted a full page, no matter what its size, and is normally assigned the page immediately following the page on which it is introduced. Every page that contains text is therefore a full page of text. This simplifies matters considerably, especially in producing draft copies for such purposes as validation and general review. (However, personal computers and desktop publishing programs have changed this.)

For purposes of draft editions, copy is often printed on only one side of the page. This, too, simplifies matters and makes it much easier for the printer.

A running sheet is not really necessary when copy is printed on one side only because all pages are printed in sequence. When copy is printed on both sides of the paper, the printer must know what page *backs* another page. The running sheet thus lists each page number (the *recto* or right-hand side, which is always an odd number) along with the number of the page that appears on the back (the *verso* or left-hand page, always an even number), and includes also the front matter pages, with their lowercase Roman numerals and the back matter, which often has special numbers, such as A-1, A-2, etc. (Manuals are not always printed page-by-page, so this can be somewhat complicated.)

Sizing Art Work

When figures are to be run in with text, the illustrations must be sized to fit the space. Mechanicals—camera-ready copy made up into pages ready for platemaking—may be of exact page size or they may be oversize. It's a common practice to use pica type (12 point or 10 pitch) and type the mechanicals on sheets approximately 20 percent oversize (11-by-14-inch repro sheets) and reduce the entire page to final print size (usually 8½-by-11 inches) when making the plates. (This improves the quality of the final product.) Either way, the illustrations must be in proportionate size when pasting them up with the type. It is also a production responsibility to reduce the size of original illustrations that are too large for direct paste-up.

Photographs are not pasted up, however, but must be copied using a screen, which breaks the photograph up into a dot pattern of varying intensity. The text of the page on which that photo is to appear is also photographed, and the negative of that screened copy is then combined with the negative of the text so a printing plate can be made of the resulting composite negative. Sizing of photographs can be done either in cropping or in screening.

PRINTING ECONOMICS

Anyone who is responsible for producing the final product—printed and bound documents—must be concerned with what the printer's processes cost and the basis on which they are priced. That requires at least a basic understanding of the printer's functions and brief explanations follow.

Types of Print Shops

There are several kinds of printers, in terms of the types of work they handle. Specialty printers are equipped for and usually specialize in turning out multipart forms and other items that require special equipment. There are also printers who specialize in complex color printing, printing of the type and quality to be found in the *National Geographic*. For purposes of this discussion we will consider, however, only those printers divided into "short-run" shops and "long-run" shops, for those are the two types of shops you are most likely to be concerned with.

Short-run shops generally turn out printing in a relatively limited number of copies, from a few dozen to a few thousand. Long-run shops turn out printing in relatively large quantities, probably 50,000 to 100,000 or more. The reason for the distinction is simple. Each type of shop has totally different—even opposite—requirements. Work done in the short-run shop is priced to reflect a great deal of labor cost because that, labor rather than equipment, is the more efficient way to do short-run work. Long-run work is the opposite: greatest efficiency is achieved by expensive equipment, rather than labor. For example, a long-run shop will use large, complicated (and expensive) presses—25-, 36-, even 48-inch presses, printing 16, 24, or 32 pages at a time and may even print both sides at the same time and turn out bound documents at the output end. The short-run shop is more likely to use a 15- or 20-inch press that prints one page at a time. A large press requires a large number of negatives to be combined to make a large plate, and of course it also requires equipment (a *plate burner*) that can make a plate that size (not to mention facilities for making up that huge composite negative). It is economical for long runs only; this shop could not begin to compete with a short-run shop for the printing of a few hundred or even a few thousand copies. And the reverse is equally true, of course; the typical short-run shop could not even handle a run of 100,000 or more, let alone do so competitively. Anyone who orders printing ought to understand this. The cost of owning and paying for a heavy equipment base can easily run up overhead to 300 percent and more, and that is reflected in the prices. The short-run of today rarely makes metal plates, any more, generally using one of the newer electrostatic platemakers, which work on the same principle as do office copiers and produce plates that are satisfactory only for short runs, but are quite inexpensive as compared with metal plates.

Charges by Printers

Many short-run print shops, especially those neighborhood copy shops who turn out very short runs and print simple line copy on offset paper or sulphite bond, charge flat rates per 100 copies. However, for longer runs and/or more complex printing, most charge by specific individual items, such as those following:

Camera work—making negatives, screened and unscreened: charge for each negative.
Plate making: charge for each plate.
Make ready: charge for mounting and adjusting each plate on the press.
Impressions: charge for impressions, usually per 1,000, unless run even shorter.

Press wash: Charge for each ink change when other than black ink
   called for.

Paper: charges vary widely, according to mill prices.

Covers: same as pages, except for paper costs and/or other special items,
   if applicable.

Drilling: cost per 1,000 holes drilling in sheets.

Trimming: cost per 1,000 sheets cut.

Staples: cost per staple, if staples used for binding.

Other binding costs: tape, punching, plastic combs, etc.

AN IMPORTANT CAVEAT

The most serious mistake made in many publications projects is clinging
to the idea that "writing" is what the project is all about and that writing
is what ought to represent the greatest part of the effort. That proves
again and again to be a grave error: Writing is the final act in creating
the manuscript. Before writing can be undertaken and carried out efficiently, ample time and effort must be devoted to all the preparatory
work—the planning, design, and research. Nor is that an entirely discrete and sequential process; it is an iterative and reiterative process,
as Figure 12–6 illustrates. For the process overall is one that cycles
and recycles, and the true hazard is the notion that early decisions and
plans must be rigidly adhered to.

Many professional writers work with a "lead," a concept that is sometimes not easy for the nonprofessional writer to understand. The lead
is the opening orientation of the manuscript. This is nominally intended
to orient the reader at the outset, according to the often-quoted homespun advice to writers and speechmakers of "Tell 'em what you're going
to tell 'em, tell 'em, and then tell 'em what you told 'em." It is a homespun
way of explaining that every presentation, whether written or vocal,
must have a beginning, a middle, and an end, or an introduction, a

FIGURE 12–6 The Iterative/Reiterative Generation Process

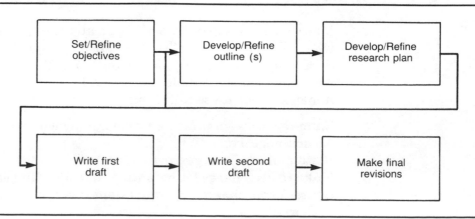

body, and a summary. However, for many professional writers—myself included—the lead must orient the writer too, for he or she cannot go on until the lead "feels right."

Professional writers, therefore, may very well discard more than a few attempted leads—because none of them feel right—before they finally find one that does feel right. That is at least partially an explanation of why the writing of most things is iterative and reiterative: the writer is seeking the lead that feels right—a lead that points the way properly and flows smoothly into the middle or main exposition. For small writing projects that may very well take the place of an outline, while for large writing projects it is ancillary to the outline.

The planning and early stages can be thought out again as a result of early research, and plans can be—and should be—updated as necessary. It is important to recognize that early plans are based on best estimates, which can be and should be revised and improved, as information accumulates.

It is my opinion that at least one half the time should be devoted to research and planning. The writing itself goes faster when the planning and research have been thorough. But even more important, the writing is more thorough and more accurate when the research and planning are adequate, and thus much less rewriting is needed.

WORD PROCESSING

Bane or boon, word processing is here to stay, and sooner or later everyone will learn to use it to gain the full and proper benefits of which it is capable and for which it was intended.

OLD DOGS AND NEW TRICKS

In the early months of World War II, while the United States was still not involved directly in the war, our government began energetically building a new and modernized army against the possibility of our being drawn into the war. It soon became clear that many of the old-time officers could not adapt to the revolutionary changes taking place in the new army and would therefore have to be retired. One observant newspaper reporter remarked, for example, that cavalry officers were still wearing spurs and carrying crops as they mounted their new steeds: armored cars and half-tracks.

The cliche about old dogs and new tricks that is still apt today in observing how many are using the modern word processors. In office after office I have observed individuals still scrawling longhand on lined yellow pads and turning the stacks of yellow paper over to modern typists, now called "word processor operators," to be keyboarded into their desktop computers and printed out as draft copy. On a few occasions when I myself worked in client's offices to help them directly in producing some important in-house publication, I was unable to gain access to a word processor and was compelled to follow the archaic pattern of scrawling my words out on yellow paper for keyboarding by a word processor operator.

Little has changed in these offices, except for retitling typists, paying them considerably more money, and gaining a modest improvement in the efficiency with which manuscripts are "typed" and "retyped" during their many development and draft stages. The result has been little or no saving in time and cost and—far more serious—no improvement at all in the writing process itself.

THE BASIC MISUNDERSTANDING OF THE WORD PROCESSOR

This reflects a serious misunderstanding—it might be more accurate to say a *lack of understanding*—of what word processing (wp) is. The inference to be drawn from this observation is that management perceives the word processor to be an investment in more efficient typing. Word processing does make revisions of draft—retyping—more efficient for skilled operators—if they are skilled enough. However, those who use word processing in this manner have, in effect, only bought themselves semiautomatic typewriters that cost from two to four times the price of good electronic typewriters, while they are paying typists considerably higher salaries. The reduction of labor and some marginal saving of time is not matched by a saving in cost. Quite the contrary, the cost is probably higher, while the true benefits do not keep pace with that higher cost.

JUST WHAT IS WORD PROCESSING?

To understand precisely what word processing is it is necessary to distinguish between hardware and software. Ignoring the relative handful of "dedicated" word processing machines (machines designed expressly for word processing and little else) that appeared early and rather briefly in the history of desktop computers, a word processor is a software program, not a hardware machine. The hardware is a computer, a machine that can do everything one would expect from a computer. It is, in many offices, dedicated to word processing because it is used exclusively or almost exclusively for that, although it can run many other programs to do many other things. Among the most popular word processors today are the granddaddy of word processors, WordStar, the new number-one seller, WordPerfect™, and many others.

Word Processing Is—or Should Be—Interactive

Word processing was an unfortunate choice of terms, although it is understandable that it was used to point clearly to a parallelism with data processing, while still distinguishing it from data processing. The term connotes a more or less mechanical function, and that is at the heart of the misunderstanding. The main usage of a big, mainframe computer is to run routine input data through detailed lengthy programs. Desktop computers and their programs—especially word processing—are different. Essentially *interactive,* a synergy takes place between human and machine when the human uses the machine interactively, rather than as a receptacle for mechanical processing. There is no such interaction or synergy when a word processor operator is entering words from a scrawled draft. For interaction to take place and synergy to result, the writer must write at the keyboard, composing on the screen and using the capabilities of the hardware and software to help produce superior writing.

A Few Distinctive Characteristics of Word Processing

Great stress has been laid on the electronic magic possible in word processing. Early advertising extolling the virtues of wp described rapturously such features as moves, global searches, global search-and-replace capabilities, and block moves to rearrange and reorganize text by shifting paragraphs, pages, and even whole chapters around. Corrections and changes by insertion and deletion are also accomplished painlessly in word processing.

These priceless features and capabilities of word processing, especially the block moves and the insert/delete capabilities, can and should be all done on-screen before printing hard copy to produce the draft. ("Printing" here refers to the output of the typewriter-like printer that is part of the word processing system.) Personally, I have made more and more extensive use of these features in my own writing. I have come to appreciate this freedom to sculpt and shape text like clay until I like what I see well enough to freeze a first model—a draft. Even for a first draft I am now able to do a great deal of rewriting and revision—even writer's sketches—before putting anything on paper, so even my first draft has had a great deal of revision, and is often more accurately my third or fourth (or even more advanced) draft.

A Few Other Advantages

There are many advantages in writing before a computer screen. Here are a few others:

■ Writer's block can be minimized. The ability to juggle text around so easily enables you to "jump start" your brain by beginning *anywhere,* even "doodling," until you have primed your mental pump and gotten it flowing.

■ Instant access to spelling aids and a thesaurus, with many modern word processors.

■ Computer "shorthand" or macros, such as those of SmartKey™, speed up the typing and the writing generally.

■ You can summon up and use your own "swipe files," files of material to which you/your organization owns the rights and which you can use freely.

■ With modern word processors, automatic compilation of a table of contents and an index. (These are chores you can assign to the wp operator.)

Who Should Input Original Text

By now it should be obvious that the philosophy here is to have the writers do the original inputting to—writing at—the computer. This is based on the consideration of interaction between user and machine—on that unprecedented freedom to manipulate ideas and their expression. It is only the writer who can use this freedom to shape and mold the text *creatively*. The word processor operator is restricted to the more or less mechanical chores, as guided by the manuscript. When the author and/or editor prepares handwritten manuscript, he or she studies the printed (typed) draft returned as proof copy, marks it up to guide the wp operator in the changes to be made, and hands it back for revision at the keyboard and printing of a new, revised draft. But in this mode the writer and editor cannot foresee some of the composition problems that wp operators will encounter. While wp operators can solve many minor problems, they do encounter problems they cannot solve because they either do not have the know how or they are unable to make the decisions required. The problems may be writing problems that must be solved by the writer or by an editor. One example of this is the case where a table is less than one page long, but happens to fall so that it straddles two pages. It must either be split in two across the two pages, an undesirable thing to do ordinarily, or moved to fit entirely on either page. Had the writer developed the copy on-screen, he or she would have encountered the problem and made whatever decision was necessary to solve it. An even more serious problem is that of an illustration that straddles two pages and cannot be split in any case but must be moved forward or back.

WP Operator Chores

This does not mean that there is not ample work for the wp operator, particularly in the latter stages, when the marked-up hard copy has been through all reviews and has been inspected by the writer and editor to be sure that all changes are grammatically and factually correct and that the directions are clear enough to guide the wp operator in making the final changes and printing the final document. In the earlier stages there is work printing out copies, maintaining files, and keeping track of things. The wp operator should maintain control of all printing and should be the only one with the capability of printing the copy to see to it that each manuscript has proper control and ID codes.

The writers, in a team writing effort, should not have access to a printer. Unless each draft is carefully coded to indicate what generation it is—first draft, second draft, third draft, on to final draft—editors and writers soon find themselves hopelessly snarled. No one knows what the latest draft is, which has been edited, and which has been reviewed. (I can report personal unhappy experience to attest to this!) Coding the manuscript by generation is not enough, for that does not indicate whether there is or is not a later generation.

To prevent this problem from arising, the following measures are recommended:

■ Place the wp operator in control of printing; no one else should have access to a printer or have a printer connected to his or her work station.
■ Put a date and time on each printout. (There are software programs that will do this automatically, if necessary.)
■ Make up a set of codes that identify the generation—first, second, third, to final—and code the manuscript files. Embed this coding in the file—possibly even in the printout while still in draft and revision stages—so the file cannot be separated from its code.
■ Add codes that identify the stage of review—editing, technically reviewed, reviewed by management—to establish absolute ID.
■ Determine which codes represent final manuscript, approved and ready for production.

These measures will give you control over the process, avoiding the confusion that can result from uncontrolled printing and circulation of draft manuscripts. You still retain all the benefits of word processing, especially those of generating the drafts at the machine. There are several other issues of importance, and a brief review of hardware and software currently in use should help, as these are representative of what is available.

THE MACHINES (HARDWARE)

Computer technology is probably the fastest-developing, fastest-changing technology of modern times, even faster than the technologies of aviation and space. IBM was a late starter in the desktop computer field, but soon dominated it and, according to their advertising, now have over three million IBM PCs placed in offices all over the world. IBM's position was so dominant in the marketplace that soon virtually all desktop computers built by others (except for Apple Computer, Inc.) were clones of the several IBM models, their basic PC (personal computer), and even those soon followed by a PC XT (extended technology PC) and a PC AT (advanced technology PC). And although IBM continued to be a prominent leader in the PC market—no one, except possibly Apple, was even a close second—in the aggregate the clones, stemming largely from Asia (Japan, Taiwan, and Korea), soon began to dominate the market, especially with the XT and AT clones. (My own XT clone is a "Made in America" clone, assembled by a small manufacturer nearby, but the major components of the system all come from those Asiatic sources.) The situation exists unchanged, so far, today, despite IBM's new models.

IBM announced its new models recently, but the consensus at the moment appears to be that they will not have a revolutionary effect since there are millions of IBM and clone computers already in place. The prognosis is, therefore, that the XTs, ATs, and their clones, along with the Apple Macintosh models, will continue to constitute the bulk of the computer population, so that obsolescence of those models is not expected to come about at an early date.

What this probably means, philosophically, is that the advance of desktop-computer technology has reached the "knee" of its curve, slowed considerably, and can be expected to grow more slowly in the future.

For the computer professionals and aficionados (nonprofessionals who are often more expert than the professionals) the new machines represent many technological advances in greater memories, higher speeds, multitasking, multiprocessing, and other capability enhancements. For the typical in-house publications and word-processing needs, these enhancements do not add a great deal; the current hardware and software systems are highly satisfactory.

Monitors

When Henry Ford was revolutionizing the automobile business with his "Tin Lizzies," he was widely quoted as saying his customers could have their automobiles in any color they wanted, as long as it was black. That could have been said for the early computer monitors—cathode ray tubes with their associated circuits—all had green screens and the square filled with lines and rows of phosphorescent green characters became a familiar symbol identifying the desktop computer.

Computer screens varied in size from five inches to nine inches to 12 inches, which became a standard for most desktop machines. Most monitors present a horizontal display, although occasionally a manufacturer offers a vertical display that presents a full-page display.

The de facto standard display is slightly less than a half-page. Computer displays are measured in lines and columns, the latter a relic of earlier computers, which dealt almost exclusively in figures. So instead of characters and/or inches of image area to describe width, as people in the publishing industry do, computer screens use *columns*. The de facto standard for word processing displays is 80 columns by 25 lines. However, one of those 25 lines is usually devoted to status—identification markings of file name, page number, and other details. Another may be devoted to a ruler line and in most cases writers work with 23 or 24 lines of copy on-screen at a time. (Standard pages are 66 lines long, with 55 lines reserved for copy, although most programs permit you to change this if you wish.)

As users began to complain of eyestrain and headaches, monitors with amber instead of green displays began to appear. These are reputedly easier on the eyes and have become rather popular.

Monitors with color screens soon became available, and are also popular today, although the color tube is considered to be somewhat inferior to monochrome (in resolution) for word processor displays.

There are many different kinds of monitors offered today, with many alleged differences, most of them technological and not easily discernible to the unaided eye. If you are about to buy a system, the best test is subjective actual trial.

Printers

Equally important is the printer in the system. Originally, there were two kinds of printers—letter-quality and draft-quality. Letter-quality machines produced typewriter-like quality, using a ball or daisywheel element with characters embossed on it. Draft-quality machines were all of the dot matrix type, using a row of pins that fashioned the letters by drawing lines, straight, curved, or angular, with dots. Daisywheel machines (most letter quality machines did use daisywheels) did not progress far, except for speed—to about 45–50 characters per second maximum—with a few refinements, such as boldface and superscripts. Dot matrix machines, on the other hand, advanced rapidly in speed and quality. Soon most of them offered a near-letter-quality option (NLQ) usually using a 9-pin printhead. Recently, 24-pin machines have appeared, and they offer full letter quality. Except for the extra-large typefaces, even under a magnifying glass the letters printed by 24-pin machines are of true letter quality.

Dot matrix machines offer great versatility of size and style in type fonts and in their ability to do graphics—draw various figures, charts, and graphs—and the popularity of daisywheel machines has waned accordingly. It is now possible to buy a good-quality 24-pin printer for less than the prices once asked for daisywheel printers and dot matrix printers of far lesser capabilities.

The latest development has been the emergence of the laser printer, a printer that uses the principles of the xerographic copying process to print hard-copy output. The office copier uses a camera to photograph an original and transfer the light pattern to a special drum or master as an equivalent pattern of electrical charges. The laser printer translates the digital information representing the computer output into a pattern of electrical charges that a laser beam then paints on the drum or master. From that point on the process is similar to that of the office copier.

Laser printers represent the most advanced printer technology. They are the most expensive printers, most of them costing thousands of dollars. (The least costly I have found, so far, was offered recently at about $1,500.)

THE PROGRAMS (SOFTWARE)

The word processor that was the best-seller for a long time was the venerable WordStar, which had been through several revisions, but none that brought about anything resembling revolutionary redesign. Ultimately, that reluctance to change—to add the many features and capabilities that became possible with the great increases in memory circuits and the growing use of the high-capacity hard disks—proved to be MicroPro's mistake. It cost MicroPro its number-one position with WordStar, as WordPerfect became the most popular word processor. But what was word processing soon became something more.

Word Processing Becomes More than Word Processing

Originally, there were two types of programs that were useful for handling language in a computer, editors and formatters. Word processors resulted from marrying these two, as the new desktop computers graduated from 4K to 16K to 32K and then to 64K memories, so that the operator could both edit and format in the same program. Ancillary programs soon came along to supplement word processors. Spelling checkers were early arrivals, successful because they not only filled a need but they were "naturals" for the work; they did just what computers were good at doing. Less popular, because the need for them was not as great and they were much more difficult to use, were programs to collect a table of contents, prepare an index, write footnotes, and help with other laborious jobs. Still other programs that were helpful were key-redefiners that created "macros"—standard phrases, paragraphs, and other such items—that could be entered into the text at the press of a key; thesauri, to help the operator find synonyms; and little utility programs that enable the operator to interrupt his or her work to jot down a note on-screen, do a calculation on-screen, hunt up a telephone number, or otherwise handle miscellaneous tasks conveniently.

As the new computers came on-stream, with 640K memories (replacing machines that tended strongly to 64K memories) and 10-, 20-, and 30-Mb hard disks became commonplace, the new generation of word processors came along with these kinds of ancillary programs integrated into them. As so many others did, I surrendered to the new trend when WordStar 4 became available. (I had, months earlier, surrendered and joined the tidal wave of 64K-machine owners converting to the new 640K machines.) Of course, many other word processors offer similar functions; I happen to be attached to WordStar simply because I started with an earlier version and I cringe at the thought of learning an entire new set of commands and reconditioning all my reflexes. Besides, I have never really agreed with the opinions of some that WordStar was overly complex. Rather, I thought that what others carped at as complexity was really versatility of functions and capabilities. In any case, if you grew up as a computer owner with a 64K machine and matching hardware, life at the keyboard changes considerably: Now, instead of leaving the program to load a spelling checker, as you would have done with the 64K machine, using this upgraded hardware and software you can invoke the spelling checker while remaining in the program. Moreover, whereas the old spelling checker simply advised you that it did not recognize a certain word and invited you to change it or accept it, the new one offers a correct spelling or perhaps several choices. All you need do is press a key; the program then makes the correction. If you have to do a little calculation while writing, a key presents a fully functional calculator on-screen, and you can do your calculation. You can even print the results out in your file, if you wish. You would also have indexing and other such conveniences, as integral parts of most modern word processors. If the telephone rings while you are working and you have one of the handy little notepad programs, you can make notes in a special window on-screen and transcribe them later, or you can look up information in some other file. You do all these things without unloading your file and without losing your place: when you are done and return to your writing, a keypress brings you back to exactly where you left the file. If you need to draw a box, the program draws it for you. And if you need to draw lines, there are keys that do that for you also. You can also generate many simple sketches on-screen, such as plots and charts. And in the next chapter we'll expand on this a bit.

Of course, most of this is wasted if you do not write at the keyboard. These are features to help you in and with the writing processes, and they are not of much use to word processor operators who are merely keyboarding what has been written by someone else.

DESKTOP PUBLISHING

It would probably not be stretching a point to regard desktop publishing as the pièce de résistance of word processing. However, the development of the technology and software so known is more a matter of degree than of kind. Probably no technology has ever sprouted new terms more rapidly or in greater profusion (and perhaps *con*fusion as well!) than the computer industry has. Some of the terms have made me a bit unhappy by their wide acceptance: You may have observed that I have made little use of the term *personal computer,* for example, preferring by far the more accurate term *desktop computer.* (*Personal computer* connotes the *use* of the machine, not its nature.) On the other hand, I find the rather new term *desktop publishing* an apt one. It does describe the activity and set the stage for it quite well. With a little imagination and a good bit of work, it is possible to create a few simple graphics with ordinary word processors and simple printers, but even more so with desktop publishing programs and modern, more sophisticated printers.

In fact, *desktop publishing* refers to both the activity itself—in essence, what we have been discussing here as "in-house publishing"—and to the software and hardware (but primarily the software) that is identified as being especially designed for and suited to the function referred to.

It is easy enough to become confused about this because (1) desktop publishing certainly appears to be nothing more than word processing decorated with a few refinements and bestowed with a new name; and (2) even the refinements are not really new, but are other, ancillary programs added to word processors. That is, these programs, word processors, font-design software, and graphics software are the direct antecedents of desktop publishing software.

Actually, desktop publishing has at least two other antecedents: The *integrated* programs, which were programs in which several programs had been combined into one, as in the case of early word processors versus later ones; and *windowing* programs, which were programs that permitted hopping about and/or combining elements of different programs by opening a "window" from the program you are in to another file or program somewhere in your system.

So all of this, combined to provide the features of word processing, graphics, multiple fonts, windows, and a few odd and assorted features in an *integrated* manner, constitute desktop publishing. There is one other factor at work here: Desktop publishing emerged and became visible approximately coincident with the emergence of laser printers, and although it is by no means established that laser printing prompted the desktop publishing idea, it certainly reinforced it. Many of those who have become the recognized experts in the field appear to operate on the premise that laser printers are an essential ingredient in desktop publishing. However, the new, 24-pin printers produce quite excellent copy too and should not be underestimated.

GRAPHIC QUALITY

Computer screens and hard-copy output devices—dot matrix printers and laser printers—create images very much as conventional printing recreates photographs: by a pattern of dots, called *pixels,* for *picture elements*. And as in conventional printing, the quality of the printed product depends on the size and number of those dots/pixels. In conventional printing the quality is a function of the number of lines in the screen through which the photograph is copied—75-line for a coarse screen, 225–line for a fine screen. Pixels are measured as totals per screen image—640 by 720—or number of dots per square inch. For example, one advertiser headlines "2,000,000 Dots Per Screen. That's What It Takes," while another claims that his system will produce 400 dpi (dots per inch) or 70,000 more dots per square inch than a laser printer produces. Of course, the printer in the system must be able to handle the quality produced by the computer. Again, there is a reasonable analogy with printing photographs—*halftones*, actually, after they have been screened—in that the paper must be capable of accepting the ink transferred by the screen: Porous, absorbent paper, such as the newsprint used for newspapers, cannot handle finely screened photographs because the ink deposited for each tiny dot in the closely compressed field of a fine screen would spread before drying and merge with the other dots, creating a blob, rather than a photograph. The fine screens are reserved to the relatively nonabsorbent smooth papers of slick magazines. So while you can easily see the individual dots of the coarse-screen halftone (often 75-line) used in a newspaper, you will find it quite difficult to distinguish them in a slick-paper magazine photograph unless you use a magnifying glass. (Thus the reason for the several different size screens used.)

There is at least one other hard-copy output device, the *plotter*. Plotters do not form and print images by dot patterns. Plotters use styli or pens to literally draw images, and the more sophisticated ones use a bank of colored pens to create outputs in color. For the most part, we are not concerned here with plotters, for they are costly devices used primarily for engineering, scientific, and similar highly technical work that requires a high degree of precision.

Chapter 13

Idea Processing

For a great many writers, especially those for whom writing is a tedious chore, idea processors have been a great boon.

THE ORIGINAL CONCEPT: AN OUTLINING TOOL

Among the more intriguing ideas in computer software has been that of programs to help you think out your ideas and build a detailed outline as you do so. The immediate objective in this concept was to furnish a convenient tool for preparing outlines, especially for those individuals who have never learned how to develop an outline properly. But it soon proved to be far more useful in that it was an idea processor—a tool to stimulate, guide, and structure thinking, with the outline almost a by-product, although it is an objective of the program.

Many individuals confuse an outline with an abstract or summary. Asked to prepare an outline for a proposed manual, they write a paragraph or two—or perhaps many paragraphs, if the subject requires it—summarizing the ideas. This does help portray a general idea and even furnishes a basis for discussion of the manual. It is not a great deal of help in directly guiding the writing of the manual or dividing the manual into its constituent parts, assigning work to a staff of writers or serving as an aid and guide to editing and reviewing manuscript drafts. It is mainly useful as a most rudimentary tool. An outline is needed that breaks the entire project down into discrete and readily discernible elements and describes in detail what will be covered in the manual. The outline must be in a form that lends itself to this. This is a form and format that should be familiar to you as one that was used in several outlines appearing in earlier chapters:

I. Main topic
   A. Secondary topic
      1. Next level of subordination
        a. Still lower subdivision

THE TRADITIONAL DIFFICULTY

The great difficulty in developing such an outline is that it is inherently an iterative process, one that can go on almost indefinitely, as you pursue your research, think out the subject, and develop your ideas. It calls for a great deal of writing and rewriting, and if you are working with paper and pencil you soon run out of space. In the manual method, you write ideas telegraphically and you leave lots of space for insertions, but there is never enough space because you rarely anticipate which items will agglutinate to the greatest degree. If for no other reason than that, outlining on a computer screen is a great help because you virtually never run out of space, if you have one of the more modern desktop computers, and you don't have to discard what you have already written to continue the expansion. That is only the beginning of the benefits that derive from computer help with this planning and outlining phase. The inherent flexibility of the medium is its greatest asset.

THE BASIC FEATURES

The basic method of developing the outline, as described and discussed here, can be done in a conventional word processor. However, the first of the two most basic features of the outlining/idea-processing programs offers a capability ordinary word processors do not: It permits you to view and/or review your developing outline at whatever level you need. Suppose that your outline has grown to the point where it has six levels of subordination and detail, and you find it difficult to gain a useful overview when confronted with a dozen or more pages and much rather minute detail. The mental gymnastics required inhibit such visualization. The idea processing software, however, enables you to view the outline at only the first level, or only the first two or three levels, or at whatever levels you wish. Perhaps you wish to see only what can be presented in a single screen. It is like having a zoom lens, permitting you to step back for the perspective of distance and scope, while still being able to zoom in on any detail when you wish to.

Figure 13–1 reproduces a portion of a generalized outline that went down to four levels of detail. Figure 13–2 shows the entire outline at the first and second levels only.

The other chief and distinguishing feature is the ability to create what some of these programs call a "leaf." That is a text breakout at whatever levels you wish to place it. That is, where you feel that a note or a paragraph of text is needed, you can insert it at the appropriate places in the outline. This is illustrated in Figure 13–3, where a portion of the outline is reproduced and shows a leaf following the last item of that portion.

The availability of these and other features has inspired the concept to evolve into one that has graduated such programs from outlining aids to thought or idea processors.

FIGURE 13–1 Portion of Original Outline

I. General maintenance philosophy.
   A. Levels of maintenance defined and discussed briefly.
      1. User or field level.
      2. Preventive/routine.
      3. Corrective.
      4. Overhaul and repair.
   B. Troubleshooting considerations.
      1. Repairable versus throwaway parts.
      2. Troubleshooting aids supplied and identified.
         a. Drawings.
         b. Charts and tables.
         c. Checklists.
   C. Maintenance history (if one exists).
      1. On earlier models/manufacturing runs.
      2. On similar items.
      3. On major components, assemblies.
   D. Maintenance projections.
      1. Engineering tests/measurements/estimates.
         a. Reliability (MTBF).
         b. Maintainability/repairability (MTTR).
      2. Other estimates.
      3. Recommended spare parts inventory.
II. Preventive/routine maintenance.
   A. Introductory instruction.
      1. General procedures and philosophy of preventive maintenance.

FIGURE 13–2 Collapsed View of Outline at Top Levels Only

I. General maintenance philosophy.
   A. Levels of maintenance defined and discussed briefly.
   B. Troubleshooting considerations.
   C. Maintenance history (if one exists).
   D. Maintenance projections.
II. Preventive/routine maintenance.
   A. Introductory instruction.
   B. Scheduled periodic inspection.
   C. Scheduled periodic cleaning and lubrication.
III. Corrective maintenance.
   A. Introductory instruction.
   B. Preliminary diagnosis.
IV. Overhaul and repair.
   A. Introductory instruction.
V. Parts and provisioning.
   A. Illustrations.

FIGURE 13–3   Text Paragraph Inserted as Leaf in Outline

---

           c. By tests and measurements.
              (1) Reference to engineering drawings.
              (2) Reference to charts and tables.
      2. Read maintenance history/reports of item, if available.
          a. Most recent routine preventive maintenance.
          b. Prior breakdowns/malfunctions.
          c. Prior parts replacements.
      3. Carry out repairs/replacements.
      4. Test for normal operation.
      5. Write report, update item maintenance record.
III. Overhaul and repair.
    A. Introductory instruction.
      1. General procedures and philosophy of overhaul and repair.
      2. Steps to be taken: cleaning, replacements of parts, rebuilding, adjustment.
      3. Basis for overhaul and repair: reports/requests submitted by other maintenance echelons.
      4. Drawings, charts, tabular data identified and invoked. *Illustrated parts breakdown, exploded-view drawings, and assembly drawings for retrofit, depot maintenance, and general O&R. Use photos also, supply parts lists and parts descriptions.*

Chapter 14

Readability Standards and Measures

If we could measure readability with true scientific precision, we could mechanize and perfect the writing of such utilitarian documents as user manuals. That is simply not possible—not yet, in any case—but a few dedicated individuals have made a good start.

READABILITY AND ITS MEASUREMENT

Dr. Rudolph Flesch has written extensively on the subject of reading and writing clearly, has developed his own method and standard for measuring a quality known as *readability,* and is regarded as an expert in the subject. Robert Gunning has also contributed to this store of knowledge, primarily with the *fog index,* a concept that assays to measure the "fog" content of writing.

This seems like a subject that ought to be a "natural" for computer application, but not a great deal has been done about it yet. However, several computer enthusiasts have attacked it—at least one refers to himself as a writer turned "techie"—and produced computer programs that attempt to measure the fog index of writing or, conversely, the readability of writing samples.

There are many problems that impede the achievement of accuracy in doing so. All such measures are based on the complexity and length of sentences and words, with some also taking into account the nature of the words as having familiar or unfamiliar referents. But formulas to enable a program to identify syllables, words, and sentences as such are approximate, at best, and their accuracy is in some proportion to the size of the sample measured—small samples generally offer a lesser degree of accuracy than lengthier samples.

THE NATURE OF READABILITY

Readability, as a measure, has little or no relation to the quality of the writing—to its validity, accuracy, adequacy, appropriateness, fluency, smoothness of expression, or any other factor normally considered as an element contributing to "good" or "poor" writing. Nor does it necessarily have anything to do with whether the writing is interesting or dull. Execrably bad writing, writing that is tedious and dull, can be highly readable. It is also true that excellent writing, even some of the classics of our literature, would score poorly on readability. Readability is only a measure of how easy or how difficult it is to *understand* the author's words and sentences. The common standard of reference is grade level, although the Flesch method utilizes a scale of numbers that do not themselves identify the estimated grade level. For example, one sample measured as 6.6 (between 6th and 7th grades) by one program is reported as a 70 by a program using the Flesch method. In another sample, using the same two programs, another sample is measured as a 6.6 also by the first program, while the second reports a Flesch number 57 for the same sample.

Writing that is judged or measured to be at junior or senior high school levels—7th to 10th grade—is generally considered to be highly readable and a good target level for almost all materials. Here are estimated reading levels of several popular periodicals, as an example:

National Enquirer	6th grade
People	7th grade
Reader's Digest	9th grade
The Wall Street Journal	11th grade

In more general terms, readability measured to be above the high school or, at least, college freshman level, is considered too high for popular consumption, even by executives and professionals. Ideally, some believe, most writing for general consumption should be at 7th to 8th grade levels.

Overall, readability measures are based on average sentence and word length. This ignores many other factors that bear on readability, such as the reader's knowledge of the subject, the organizing of ideas, the use of tables and illustrations, the number of concepts the reader is asked to absorb, and the complexity or simplicity of the sentence structure. It also ignores the strangeness or familiarity of the words used—for a polysyllabic word that is familiar is more readable than a monosyllabic word that is strange or rare. While you should strive to achieve maximum readability through simple and straightforward sentences, short words, and other such methods, you should also employ all the other means available to help the reader follow your meaning with minimum of effort. Readability and understandability are not the same thing, and the two should not be confused with each other. Still, readability measures have a place and are a help, as long as we recognize their limitations. There are several computer programs that can help. Two that I reviewed measure a text and report its measure. A third one is somewhat more sophisticated: It offers help in making the text more readable by identifying difficult words, words that contribute to fog, and the program suggests alternative words in vocabulary lists that are part of the program.

The simplest program I have encountered is READ, which simply asks for the name of the file to be read, and then reports a figure and a verbal estimate of difficulty, such as "college junior" or "professional person."

A little more sophisticated is PC-READ, which presents a graphically illustrated scale of grade levels, running from grade 5 to 18, on which it indicates the estimated readability of the file it has analyzed. This program also offers alternative methods for measuring, including periodic sampling of an entire manuscript.

The most advanced such system that I have encountered to date—has been one named MAXI-READ. All of these programs are "shareware" (explanation of this to follow), rather than typical commercial products. These are excellent tools to help writers and editors achieve higher degrees of readability than many user manuals now achieve. Best of all, these programs are almost absurdly inexpensive. Moreover, you can try them out at no cost!

ELECTRONIC BULLETIN BOARDS AND "SHAREWARE"

In the world of computers there is a phenomenon known as the "BBS,"—electronic bulletin board systems. There are literally thousands of these in operation; many are on a purely commercial basis and offer information—public databases—and other services for fees of various kinds. But there are also many hobbyist-type BBSs, operated at their personal expense by enthusiasts who usually do not accept fees (although many gratefully accept voluntary donations). When they do charge, the fee is quite modest, virtually nominal.

They compile large inventories of software—computer programs. A few of these programs are in the public domain, but most are generally referred to as "shareware." Everyone is invited to try these programs without charge and, if they like them well enough, add them to their own inventories of regularly used programs. Users are asked to donate a modest suggested amount and pay a small fee to register their ownership. Shareware programs are not in the public domain; the authors of these programs hold copyrights to them. While private individuals are expected to make donations and pay registration fees entirely as a voluntary act, the authors are consistently firm in demanding that commercial users must register their ownership. MAXI-READ is such a program. You can download (copy) it and the others from a BBS over your telephone line if you are equipped with a modem and suitable communications software, or you can order it directly from the publishers, whose names and addresses are furnished in the Bibliography. MAXI-READ is probably best explained in a brief summary from the manual that accompanies the program. That summary is reproduced through the permission of the authors, RWS & Associates, Pro Form-ance, of San Francisco, California (whose address appears later in the Bibliography).

To see how MAXI-READ can be useful, consider the sentence below. It came from a recent instruction booklet from the IRS on filling out your federal 1040 tax form. It was found in a section titled: "Questions For Employers Who Provide Vehicles For Use By Employees."

"For employers providing vehicles to their employees, a written policy statement regarding the use of such vehicles, if initiated and kept by the employer, will relieve the employee of keeping a separate set of records for substantiation requirements."

MAXI-READ's Analysis of This Sentence

Overall Readability	*Grade Level (12 – High School)*	*Flesch Index (0 – Low, 100 – High)*	*Number of Words/ Sentence (15 – Low, 7 – High)*
Very Low	18	21	38

Note first that the IRS's sentence is not a question as the title of the section implied. But, more to the point, the sentence is unnecessarily complex and hard to understand.

The IRS's sentence reflects the writing style found, until recently, in many business, government, and school settings. The attitude seemed to be: The longer the sentence, the better they work. The more long, complicated words you use, the more impressed your audience will be.

But values are changing. Thanks partly to the work of people like Rudolf Flesch and Robert Gunning, writing is now being judged more on how effective it is than by the number of long words it contains. Effective means: Did the message get through? Did it have an impact? Did we get the results we wanted?

READABILITY ASSISTANCE

The program goes beyond measurement and evaluation, and offers assistance in the form of (1) a list of polysyllabic words found in the sample, and (2) a long list of synonyms you can summon up to help you find simpler words to replace the lengthy ones.

ILLUSTRATIONS

Perhaps better illustrations of how MAXI-READ works are shown in Figures 14–1 and 14–2, where two of the program evaluations are reproduced. If you read the measures and reports of polysyllabic words and long sentences and how that affects readability estimates, you can begin to understand the philosophy of the method. Note, too, that grade levels, a commonly used measure and indicator of reading difficulty, are assigned the samples and their measures.

**FIGURE 14–1 MAXI-READ Output for Sample Text and
Interpretation Help**

```
======================== MAXI-READ   Summary ========================
 Readability   VERY LOW       LOW       AVERAGE       HIGH     VERY HIGH
 Summary::::  |_____+_____+_____■_+_____+_____|

    Approximate GRADE LEVEL:   10       +---[   Index Summary   ]---+
          The FLESCH INDEX:    58    L  0|_____+_____+___■__+_____|100 H
 Personal Tone-% Personal Words:  4   O  0|_____+____■_+_____+_____|10  I
   Percent SESQUIPEDALIAN WORDS:  11  W 15|___■__+_____+_____+_____|0   G
 Average # of WORDS PER SENTENCE: 23    18|■_____+_____+_____+_____|7   H
 Average # of SYLLABLES PER WORD: 1.5  2.5|_____+_____+___■__+_____|1.0

 # of 'SENTENCES':   9      # of WORDS:   208   Total # of SYLLABLES:   307

 SESQUIPEDALIAN WORDS   |  The Following Words may be ADDING TO COMPLEXITY.
                        |Maximum Shown:  250 Words/13 Char. per Word|

MAXI-READ     ENHANCEMENTS   MAXI-READ     substantially  immediately
Exceptions    abbrevia-3     convenience   consolidated   PowerTyping
PowerTyping   tremendous     flexibility   MAXI-READ.     suggestions
```

Courtesy RWS Associates/Pro-Formance

FIGURE 14-2   Another MAXI-READ Screen and Part of Synonym List

```
================================ MAXI-READ  Summary ================
 Readability   VERY LOW      LOW        AVERAGE      HIGH      VERY HIGH
 Summary::::  |_____+___█___+_____+_____+_____|

    Approximate GRADE LEVEL:  15      +---[   Index Summary   ]---+
        The FLESCH INDEX:     42   L   0|_____+_____█_+_____+_____|100 H
 Personal Tone-% Personal Words: 1   O   0|___█_+_____+_____+_____|10  I
    Percent SESQUIPEDALIAN WORDS: 22  W  15|█____+_____+_____+_____|0   G
 Average # of WORDS PER SENTENCE:  7     18|_____+_____+_____+___█_|7   H
 Average # of SYLLABLES PER WORD: 1.8   2.5|_____+___█_+_____+_____|1.0

  # of 'SENTENCES':   17      # of WORDS:   134    Total # of SYLLABLES:   247

  SESQUIPEDALIAN WORDS  |  The Following Words may be ADDING TO COMPLEXITY.
                        |Maximum Shown:  250 Words/13 Char. per Word|
```

development   Complexity   applications Corrective   Characteristi
technologies   procedures   Installation Functional   PRELIMINARY
PRELIMINARY   Multi-volume   Technology/te complexity   delivered
Unassembled   installation   adjustment   INSTRUCTIONS   DOCUMENTATION
Schematics

WORD	SYNONYM(S)	WORD	SYNONYM(S)
Abandon	Desert, Leave	Confederate	Ally
Abbreviate	Cut, Shorten	Conspicuous	Visible, Clear
Accelerate	Hurry, Speed up	Contaminate	Infect, Pollute
Acceptable	Pleasing, Welcome	Contemplate	Look at, Consider
Accident	Mishap	Convenient	Fit, Useful
Accomodate	Adapt, Fit, Suit	Conversation	Talk, Speech
Accomplish	Do, Finish	Demonstrate	Show, Prove
Acknowledge	Admit, Allow	Derivation	Source
Adjacent	Next to, Near	Deteriorate	Decay, Lessen
Advantageous	Good	Determine	Decide, Find out
Alternative	Choice, Option	Duplicate	Copy
Amalgamation	Union, Group	Economical	Frugal, Saving
Ambiguous	Vague, Unclear	Educate	Train, Teach
Anticipation	Hope	Effervescent	Bubbly
Appropriate	Fitting, Suited	Elementary	Easy, Simple
Approximate	About	Eliminate	Get rid of, Omit
Capricious	Odd, Fickle	Elucidate	Clarify, Explain
Combination	Mixture, Union	Embellish	Enhance, Adorn
Comfortable	Pleasant	Employment	Work, Job
Communicate	Write, Tell, Say	Encourage	Urge, Support
Compensation	Payment, Reward	Encumbrance	Load, Burden
Competent	Able, Fit	Endeavor	Try, Attempt
Comprehend	Know, Grasp	Enormous	Immense, Huge

Glossary

We live in a world full of strange and exotic jargon—special terms and idiom used within each profession and peculiar to that profession. We have been discussing two worlds, the world of computers and that of publications and printing. Here are some of the most common of those terms—those that are current at the time of this writing, for they change rapidly, especially in the dynamic computer industry. But even in publications and printing a great many new terms have evolved from the changes brought about by the effects of offset printing, new office machines, word processors, and desktop publishing. To make matters even worse, many terms have more than one meaning, depending on who is using the term and in what connection it is being used. You will run into such terms as *hacker* and *crash* when chatting with computer enthusiasts, which different people use to mean slightly different things. Even the well-established term *word processor* is used to refer to both the hardware and the software used for the purpose. And perhaps you never thought of paper as a hard substance, but in the computer world the paper output of the printer is known as *hard copy*. In any case, here is a glossary of terms you are most likely to encounter and need to understand in the course of turning out user manuals, dealing with printing needs, and working with computers, word processing, and desktop publishing.

alphanumeric Adjective generally, referring to use of both letters and numerals, as in alphanumeric character set, alphanumeric codes, etc.

annotate Practice of placing notes to explain or elaborate on text passages.

archive Storage or backup copy of files.

automatic pagination Word processor function of recognizing each new page and placing folio (page number) there, as ordered by program or your special command.

backup "Insurance" copy on separate disk or tape.

baud, baud rate In practical terms, rate at which data bits are sent/received in bits per second; used especially with reference to communications via modem and telephone.

bidirectional (printing) Ability/ action of printers to print in both directions.

bird-dog To monitor, administer, and generally "stay on top" of all details of publications project, especially one with "short fuse" (pressing deadline).

bleed Printing that runs to edge of page and "bleeds off," usually a solid ink block or illustration; both noun and verb.

block Section of text, treated as unit, for word processing functions.

block move Word processor function of moving entire block of text.

blow-up Photographic enlargement or enlarging process (both noun and verb).

boilerplate Standard or stock information, which may be pasted up in more than one document, both physically and electronically.

boldface Heavy typeface, available as separate font of most type families, available in many word processing programs as a special printer function.

buffer Storage device, usually for temporary storage of data to free up computer, as in case of printer buffer, used to compensate for inability of printers to keep up with rate at which computer supplies data.

burn Process of making metal printing plate from negative by exposing plate, through negative, to strong light in "plate burner"; also extended to refer to other ways in which printing plates are made, such as electrostatic or xerographic process.

byte Group of digital bits processed as a group, currently 8 bits, representing one alphanumeric character.

camera-ready Any materials in final condition and ready to be photographed for plate-making; applied to assembled final copy, but also to any materials which are ready to be made up as part of pages, without preliminary processing; also referred to as *camera copy.*

cathode ray tube (CRT) Tube with screen for displaying data of all types with phosphorescent illumination; same type of tube, generally, as that used for TV.

center head Headline or caption that is centered, instead of starting flush left.

character Individual letter, numeral, symbol, or diacritical mark; one byte in word processors.

chip Functional electronic element consisting of entire circuit or set of circuits etched into tiny sliver or wafer of silicon.

coated paper Paper made with coatings, such as clay, to make it dense and extra smooth, so as to present sharp, well-defined printing.

cold type Type set by strike-on (impact) or photo-typesetting methods; non-metal type.

color registration Process of aligning plates to print different colors in correct positions or "registration" with each other.

color separation Process of preparing camera-ready copy for printing in more than one color by providing separated copy for each color ink.

composite negative Photo negative containing both line copy and screened or halftone copy, stripped together or mounted together on goldenrod with a "window" for the halftone.

comprehensive Short form of *comprehensive layout,* a detailed diagram of precisely where each bit of copy and other elements will fit in final mechanical.

contributor A freelancer who sells original material to a publication.

copy Material for publication; generally applies to text material, although sometimes meaning is extended to cover other material, which may be rough (unedited draft) or final (edited/revised) draft or camera-ready material.

copy fitting Process of making copy fit space by various means, such as finding enough space for it or cutting/trimming it to fit.

cps Characters per second, measure of rate at which printer operates.

crash Refers to loss of data, collapse of program, power failure, other such disaster; similar in meaning to older term *dump,* which also referred to loss of data, as well as display of compiled program.

crop marks Marks on board bearing mounted photograph to show photographer/platemaker which portion of print is to be printed and which to be omitted or "cropped out."

cropping Marking photo or other illustration to show printer which portion is to be printed.

cropping Act of marking photo with crop marks, especially making editorial judgments for cropping.

cursor Symbol on screen, showing where next action will take place or, conversely, moved by operator to direct computer program to site of next action.

daisywheel Printing element used in many letter-quality printers; type of printer.

database Bank of related information.

database manager Computer program used to manage, manipulate, process filed/stored data.

disk Metal or plastic disk coated with magnetic oxide and serving as storage medium. (See also *floppy.*)

dele Mark, comment to order deletion.

desktop publishing Latest developments in use of desktop computers for creating copy for publishing; also software programs used for purpose, integrating word processing, graphics, and other techniques.

dot matrix Method of printing wherein characters are formed by series of dots; dot matrix printer.

double pass Action of dot matrix printhead going over character twice to achieve near letter quality or otherwise improve quality.

download Receive files from another computer via modem and telephone connection.

dpi Abbreviation for dots per inch, a measure of resolution on screen or in printout.

dropout Tendency of some copy to fade in photography or plate-making, especially large areas of solid blacks and fine details. Applies also to dropout of light blue, seen by camera as white and used deliberately for the purpose.

dummy Mock-up of final product, used for study and evaluation or to guide someone, as in printer's dummy. (See *printer's dummy.*)

dump Presentation of file or program (usually on screen) in hexadecimal code, with or without alphanumeric text.

editor, text editor Portion of word processor program responsible for entering, correcting, manipulating text; also individual who reviews and corrects manuscript copy.

em, em dash An *em* is the width of the capital M of any type font, and an *em dash* is of the same width. For typewriters and most printers, use a double hyphen for em dash.

en One-half an em.

ENTER/RETURN Both are used to enter commands and, usually, to start a new paragraph.

file Set of related records in storage or in work, identified by unique name; may be of any size, at operator's choice.

floppy Colloquial for floppy disk or diskette, a flexible plastic disk, encased in a paper sleeve, 3, 3-1/2, 5-1/4, or 8 inches in diameter, used to store data on its magnetic coating.

folio Page number; also report or other brief document.

follow copy Editorial instruction to reproduce copy exactly as shown, despite apparent misspellings or other errors.

font Entire set of type characters, including numerals and symbols. Sometimes applied to entire "type family," which includes other fonts, such as italics, boldface, small capitals, and special symbols.

foot, footing Special copy appearing at bottom of page, such as *running foot,* a notice, title, or slogan appearing at foot of each page.

form Paper form used to facilitate paste-up and layout. Usually represents a single page or two-page spread. Completed form is then camera-ready—mechanical—final copy, ready for plate making. Term is linear descendant of metal-type days, when *form* was literally a metal frame holding type.

format Design of publication, including type style, layout, other characteristics.

formatter Portion of word processor that permits operator to organize/reorganize copy for printer or other output peripheral device and/or issue instruction to the output device.

global search [and replace] Refers to ability of word processors to find any/all references/uses of a word or term and, if ordered, to replace that word/term with another.

goldenrod Yellow paper forms used in print shops for mounting negatives for making metal plates.

graphics Drawings, other illustrations (although printing is itself one of the graphic arts); in word processing refers to ability of computer systems and programs to generate drawings of many kinds.

gutter White space between columns of type in two- or three-column copy; (inside margins between pages in single-column copy).

halftone Photograph or other continuous-tone material converted to dot pattern for printing; also applied to screen used to convert copy to dot or halftone pattern and to resulting negative and plate.

hard copy Printed copy, as distinct from screen display or "soft copy."

head, heading Abbreviation for *headline* as in *sidehead* and *center head.* Also title, notice, slogan appearing at top of page, as in *running head* (when it appears on every page).

headliner Machine for creating headline-size type in strips using photographic process.

headnote Note appearing at top of page, usually used only with tabular data.

hexadecimal Number system of base 16, used in computers for many purposes.

imprinting Printing over surface already printed or printing in space reserved for purpose during prior printing; see also overprinting and surprinting.

insert Editorial meaning: copy to be added by insertion in text (done electronically in word processors).

I/O Stands for Input/Output, controls and information transfer in computers.

justification Condition of left- and/or right-hand edges of lines in alignment, resulting in absolutely even margins; generally accomplished by adjusting spacing between words, letters, or both. Most word processors can justify automatically. Also called *right justification* and *justified right* because left justification is taken for granted.

kerning Refers to tightening spaces between characters, especially tucking small characters partially under initial capitals.

kilobyte (Kb) 1024 bytes; each byte equals one alphanumeric character; standard page of double-spaced typed copy equals approximately 2Kb or (more commonly) 2K.

laser printer Printer that uses laser and principle of xerographic office copiers to produce hard copy.

layout Plan for organizing copy and illustrations; actual design sketch or plan for doing so; design itself; can be preliminary (rough layout) or final (comprehensive layout).

line copy Any copy that does not require halftone screening; usually includes all text, tables, and line drawings, such as graphs, charts, and engineering sketches.

line drawing Drawing that consists of lines and other black and white contrast, without shades between the two (see also *tone*).

line negative Negative of line copy.

logo Abbreviation for *logotype;* a distinctive symbol, stylized letter or word, or other unique designation of identity; usually a registered trademark.

make-ready Installation of printing plate and adjustment of press to begin printing; a specific item charged by most printers as a separate item.

make-up Assembling and preparing all camera-ready material to create the mechanicals from which printing will be done.

mask Rectangle of black or red paper/plastic pasted on camera-ready copy where photo will appear to create "window" in negative for making composite negative.

mechanical Complete final page or multi-page spread ready for platemaking and printing.

memory Internal circuits of computer that store information, generally on a temporary basis, usually known as RAM (random access memory) in small computers.

modem Term derived from *modulator-dem*odulator, a device that enables computers to communicate (transfer data) over telephone lines.

monitor Usually refers to "soft copy" or "soft display," represented by CRT (cathode ray tube) screen, liquid crystal display, or other such presentation, as distinct from "hard copy" printed output.

mortise Practice of making corrections to camera-ready copy by actually cutting defective material out and replacing it with correction copy—splicing the correction copy in; also called *splicing*; also used to combine screened negative with line negative to form composite negative, in which case it is called "stripping."

nameplate Headline/title block of newsletter, other periodical, usually at top of front page.

offset Colloquialism for modern offset printing processes and related items, such as "offset plates," "offset presses," "offset paper," etc.; also refers to undesired transfer of ink from freshly printed surface to other surface, such as back of another sheet.

online Refers to database/information services available via modem-telephone connection and communication and to communication process itself.

opaque Paint out defects with white substance on paper, dark substance on photographic negatives.

overprinting Printing one character on top of another; printing on top of already printed surface; also called surprinting (see *surprinting*); imprinting (see *imprinting*); also used to create special characters not available in type font.

page display Word processing term for displaying entire page on screen or for showing where page begins and ends to help operator fit copy.

paste-up Act of pasting up copy, as prescribed by comprehensive; copy that has been pasted up.

photocomposition Copy composed by phototypesetting.

photo-direct Platemaking by xerographic and other devices that create printing plates (usually paper or plastic, rather than metal) without the intermediate stage of a negative.

pitch Number of characters and spaces per linear inch—e.g., 10 pitch = 10 characters per inch.

pixel Contraction of *picture element,* and measure of resolution or ability to present detail on monitor screen; analogous to halftone dots for printing photographs.

plotter Device for making hard copy graphics from computer output using pens or styli; most effective way to do so.

printer Typewriterlike machine for making hard copy printouts of computer data; daisywheel, dot matrix, or laser type, (see *laser printer*).

printer's dummy Mock-up of publication to guide printer in making up small publications, such as brochure (or when special requirements must be explained); for larger publications, a running sheet is more appropriate. (See *running sheet.*)

process color Color printing of continuous-tone material, such as color photos.

proportional spacing Allotting horizontal space for each type element according to width of the element, instead of allowing the same space for each.

ragged right Opposite of right-justified.

RAM Random access memory; device that constitutes memory for most small computers, and is what is generally referred to by such designations as "64k computer" or "16k" memory, which denote capacity of RAM.

read-only memory Designated as ROM, refers to internal device (microchip) with fixed program which cannot be changed, containing instruction set for computer.

read-write Indicates ability to read what is stored and/or write—add to or change what is written there—as in case of RAM; used as adjective to designate "read-write head" and other components which permit read-write functions.

reduction Opposite of blow-up: reduction in size by photographic means.

registration Alignment of elements on page, especially of pages which must go through the press more than once for successive printings.

registration marks Guides on copy to help printer in getting proper registration of printed material.

resolution Ability of monitor screen and/or printer to present detail clearly, usually as a consequence of number of pixels or dots per character block or square inch; partly dependent on hardware quality and partly on software; see also dpi.

roman, roman types Whole class of typefaces, with serifs and other characteristics.

rough Refers to preliminary—rough—layout and, also, to preliminary sketch.

rub-downs, rub-down type Colloquialisms for decal type.

rubylith Red plastic film used to mask photographs in camera-ready copy and so create a window for combining line and halftone negatives in a composite.

runaround Type/text set to permit space, usually of irregular shape or different than normal column width, for tables or illustrations.

running foot See *foot.*

running head See *head.*

running sheet Form instructing printer how to print the publication, especially in specifying which pages print one-side only and which are "backed up" (printed on both sides). (See also *printer's dummy.*)

sans serif Without serifs, as in Helvetica types.

screen Face of CRT, in word processing hardware references, and to display, in software references; also used, in publications and printing, to refer to device used to break photo up into pattern of dots and to action of so doing.

screen back Act of using screens, even for line copy, in some cases, to create special effects of [apparent] differences in tone.

screened negative Negative of photo made through screen; also referred to as halftone negative.

search and replace See *global search [and replace]*.

self-mailer Mailing piece—brochure, newsletter, other—which has address box on outside and does not require envelope or wrapper to be mailed.

sidehead Headline that begins flush left.

software Programs and other computer instructions which may be changed readily.

spelling checker Program that includes dictionary and reviews words for spelling; many are designed to permit additions by user.

splice See *mortise*.

spooler Buffer device, used to store information temporarily to permit computer to do other work while printer is operating. (See also *buffer*.)

stet Editorial direction to "let it stand" as it was originally (before editorial change).

strip Splicing line and halftone negatives together to form composite negative.

sulphite bond Paper made of wood pulp, but resembling rag bond paper.

surprinting Printing over already printed surface. (See *overprinting*; also see *imprinting*.)

T/C Common abbreviation for Table of Contents.

tint block Technique of printing block of light color, usually by "screening back," and overprinting in other color.

tone Material used by illustrators to create special effects, such as shading, somewhat resembling effects of screening.

upload Opposite of download; to send file to another computer via modem and telephone connection.

window Transparent area in negative created by using *mask* in camera ready copy, so that *composite negative* can be made up with splicing negatives; also area of computer screen in which portion of another file or program can be seen.

word processor Software programs used to write, edit, and format copy by computer; also used sometimes to refer to hardware.

Bibliography of References and Ancillary Sources

There are many excellent sources of additional information on the subjects discussed in these pages. The listings offered here are typical of what is available, but are far from complete. Rather, it is a starter list. Other than the general grouping of the items there is no significance to the order in which they appear.

WRITING, FOR BUSINESS AND IN GENERAL

Janis J. Harold, and Howard R. Dressner. *Business Writing*. Barnes & Noble Books, 1956.

Fielden, John S., Ronald E. Dulek, and Jean D. Fielden. *Elements of Business Writing*. Englewood Cliffs, N.J.: Prentice-Hall, 1984.

Holtz, Herman. *Word Processing for Business Publications*. New York: McGraw-Hill, 1985.

Bernstein, Theodore. *The Careful Writer*. New York: Atheneum, 1965.

Weisman, Herman. *Technical Report Writing*. Merrill, 1966.

Holtz, Herman. *The Consultant's Guide to Proposal Writing*. New York: John Wiley & Sons, 1986.

Newman, Edwin. *On Language*. Warner Books, 1980.

Strunk, William, Jr., and E. B. White. *The Elements of Style*. New York: Macmillan, 1972.

DESKTOP PUBLISHING

Makuta, Daniel J., and William F. Lawrence. *The Complete Desktop Publisher*. Greensboro, N.C.: Compute! Publications, Inc., 1986.

Bove, Tony, Cheryl Rhodes, and Wes Thomas. *The Art of Desktop Publishing*. New York: Bantam Books, 1986.

PERIODICALS

Publish!, PCW Communications, Inc.
PC Publishing, Hunter Publishing Company, Inc.

SOFTWARE AND SUPPLIERS

There is a superabundance of software offered commercially. The following is therefore only a sampling of what is available. The divisions are somewhat arbitrary in that many programs today have multiple capabilities and may combine such programs and capabilities as word processing, idea and outline processing, graphics, key redefining, and desktop publishing.

KEY REDEFINERS

Smartkey™, Soft-ware Research Technologies.
ProKey™, RoseSoft, Inc.

WORD PROCESSORS

WordStar®, MicroPro® International Corporation.
WordPerfect™, Satellite Software International.
Framework, Ashton-Tate®.
MS Word™, Microsoft® Corporation.

DESKTOP PUBLISHING PROGRAMS

The Newsroom Pro™, Springboard Software, Inc.
ClickArt Personal Publisher™, Software Publishing Corporation.
Fontasy™, ProSoft®.
FormWorx™, Analytx International, Inc.
Page Maker®, Aldus Corporation.
Harvard™ *Presentation Graphics,* Software Publishing Corporation.
DeskSet™, G.O. Graphics, Inc.
HotShot®, Symsoft.

IDEA/OUTLINE PROCESSORS

Ready™, Living Videotext, Inc.

READABILITY MEASUREMENT

MAXI-READ 2.0, RWS & Associates, 132 Alpine Terrace, San Francisco, CA 94117.

PC-READ 2.5, Joey Robichaux, Wash 'n' Ware Software Products, P.O. Box 91016-199, Baton Rouge, LA 70821.

READ 2.1, A Program to Calculate Flesch Readability Scores, Glenn Spiegel, 4821 Morgan Drive, Chevy Chase, MD 20815.

Index